HITLE

& JAPAN

THE HOLLO

ALLIANC

HITLER & JAPAN: THE HOLLOW ALLIANCE

Johanna Menzel Meskill

Atherton Press
New York
1966

Address all inquiries to:
Atherton Press
70 Fifth Avenue
New York 10011

Library of Congress
Catalog Card Number: 66-20833

FIRST EDITION

Manufactured in
the United States of America
Designed by Mel Byars

For My Mother

Acknowledgments

Initially, my interest in this subject stemmed from the common urge to find the general pattern behind stray childhood memories and experiences. In my case, these included a youth spent in wartime Germany and, more particularly, memories of Japanese victories traced in geography classes; of school reports happily registering the fall of some British or American outpost to Japan, and of visits to cultural functions in honor of our wartime ally. My curiosity soon outran this early context, of course, but a link remained between the sights and sounds of those days and the present inquiry. I therefore dedicate this book to my mother, who first taught me, among many things, skepticism toward the aims and rhetoric of Nazi Germany.

Like so many books, this one started as a doctoral dissertation and has been recast and refined over the years. I am grateful to my two *Doktorväter*, Donald F. Lach of The University of Chicago, and Earl H. Pritchard, now of the University of Arizona, for their guidance on the dissertation. Informal but invaluable advice at this early stage came also from Gerhard L. Weinberg, now at the University of Michigan.

On matters of interpretation and style, I have benefited from my colleagues at Vassar College, Evalyn

A. Clark, Charles C. Griffin, and Alma Luckau Molin. Colonel Thomas Everett Griess of the Unites States Military Academy at West Point gave assistance on some technical questions. Elaine Bjorklund of Vassar's geography department designed the map.

For access to special material in their custody and for an opportunity to discuss it with them, I am grateful to James W. Morley of Columbia, Louis Morton of Dartmouth, and Paul R. Sweet of the State Department.

During 1955–56, I enjoyed the support of the American Association of University Women who awarded me the Dorothy Bridgman Atkinson Fellowship. Vassar College gave small grants for summer research and clerical expenses. To both, I extend my thanks.

No less important has been the generous and cheerful assistance extended by the staffs of libraries, offices, and archives. Without their resourcefulness in locating material that I was not allowed to "browse" for, this work could not have been completed. I remember in particular Mr. Dean Allard and his staff in the Office of Naval History; Mr. Philip Brower and his staff at the Document Center in Alexandria, Va.; Dr. Dagmar Perman who, while supervising the filming of German captured records, offered numerous valuable leads to sources; and Mr. Finke at the Office of the Chief of Military History who extended similar help.

John Meskill read the final draft of the manuscript and suggested numerous improvements of substance and style.

JOHANNA MENZEL MESKILL

Vassar College
March 1966

Contents

THE PURSUIT OF THE GREAT COALITION

1

Alliances between sovereign states are surely among the least stable of political associations. Despite professions of fidelity and common purpose, most alliances have been effective for only short periods of time and only as long as it suited the interests of their signatories. As for the German-Japanese alliance of World War Two, the old saw that an alliance was a "marriage of convenience" expressed only half the shocking truth. It was more like a long and uneasy engagement, maintained long past the hope of eventual union, not because the partners had become comfortably used to each other, but because breaking the engagement would have reduced the prestige of each in the neighborhood.

Germany and Japan each found the existence and policies of the other convenient, to be sure, but the limited benefit which each derived from the other neither depended on their formal alliance nor was enhanced by it. Beyond the simple fact that both powers during roughly the same period challenged the international order as established at the great post-World War One conferences of Versailles and Washington, nothing united Germany and Japan. Even while they shared some of the same opponents, the German and the Japanese antagonism toward Britain, *or* the United States, *or* Russia involved such different objects of contention and such different questions of timing that a coordination of German and Japanese policies did not follow automatically from the fact of their common opposition to other powers.

Germany and Japan, moreover, were caught in such delusions about each other's political and military goals and practiced such secrecy and deception concerning their own objectives that even on those few occasions when their interests genuinely converged they were unable to coordinate their policies. The conclusion of the Tripartite Pact itself and the first fifteen months of the pact (September 1940 to December 1941) proved that in the crucial area of political and military coordination the alliance was ineffective from the start and that what then seemed to the outside world like the establishment of a common conspiracy against the peace was merely a fortuitous meeting of two lines of force, crisscrossing in the pursuit of different objectives. These lines intersected only twice, once in September 1940, when the Tripartite Pact was concluded, and again in December 1941, when Japan and Germany within three days of each other declared war on the United States. Before, between, and after these dates the allies aimed at different and often incompatible ends, often deceiving each other and themselves into the bargain.

Yet they searched, tortuously, for an alliance. Their aims and the shifting meanings which the two governments read into their alliance, especially in 1940 and 1941, are discussed in this chapter. Chapter Two takes up the story of German-Japanese relations at a time, after December 1941, when both powers were allies in a common war.

GREAT EXPECTATIONS

On the German side, Adolf Hitler had in the 1930s looked upon Japan as a potential ally in a German-Soviet conflict. Contrary to informed opinion in the Reichswehr, he believed that a Japanese attack on Siberia would greatly benefit Germany in such a war.[1] Perhaps his earliest image of Japan—the victor over Russia in 1904–1905, whom he had cheered as an Austrian schoolboy—had continued to shape

Hitler's thought. His own analysis of strategic errors in World War One suggested that encirclement had been Germany's undoing. In any future war, Hitler meant to keep Germany's "back free" while himself encircling her opponents. By the 1930s, an ideological disguise for the rapprochement of the two powers was available. Just as the Comintern stood in fact for the Soviet government, the German-Japanese anti-Comintern pact of November 1936 amounted to an anti-Russian alliance. Its secret protocols provided for benevolent neutrality, should one of the signatories be at war with the Soviet Union, and looked toward military cooperation against Moscow.[2]

The anti-Russian orientation remained a link between Berlin and Tokyo after 1936, when new enemies tended to drive Germany and Japan more closely together. As both nations again challenged the *status quo*—through the China Incident and the Anschluss—both came into growing opposition to the Western powers who defended the postwar order. Japan clashed with Great Britain and the United States, Germany with Great Britain and France.

Germany's calculations in regard to Japan assumed a new dimension in 1938. She now began to think of Japan not merely as a counterweight against the Soviet Union but also as an ally against her Western opponents, who were thought to be vulnerable because of their colonial holdings in Asia. It is difficult to date precisely when Hitler himself began to think in these terms. In the famous secret speech of November 1937 in which he outlined his plans for war, Japan still figured only as a counterpoise against Russia.[3] Hitler recognized that Japan's expansion in the Far East had played into his hands because it threatened the interests of his opponents, England

and France, and forced them to disperse their forces, but he evidently did not expect Japanese pressure to be strong enough to deter the two from interfering with his own plans in Europe.

By early 1938, however, Japan was being cast in this new role as counterweight against Hitler's Western opponents. The idea first appeared in a memorandum submitted to Hitler by Joachim von Ribbentrop, German ambassador to London, who was soon to become foreign minister. It may very well have been Hitler's own brainchild. Ribbentrop's memorandum posed the question of how to ensure French and British neutrality at the time when Germany would alter by force the *status quo* in Central Europe. The key, as Ribbentrop saw it, was British neutrality, because without Britain France would not aid her ally Czechoslovakia or the Austrians. The aim of German diplomacy, as Ribbentrop sketched it in early 1938, was a situation in which

> England—because of insufficient armament or because of the threat to her empire by a superior coalition of powers (for instance, between Germany, Italy, and Japan) tying down her military forces elsewhere—could not give France sufficient support in Europe.[4]

To serve Germany's ends, Ribbentrop argued, the projected alliance must be tightly knit, and no doubt must be allowed to remain in the minds of the enemy that to engage one of the signatories was to engage them all. As Ribbentrop pointed out:

> To be sure, this coalition would have to be very closely united, and England and France must have no reason to doubt that Italy and Japan are supporting us firmly, and that, if necessary, the joint forces of the coalition would be employed in a lightning blow.

Through the spring of 1938, Ribbentrop indulged in a series of pro-Japanese gestures that were meant to prepare the atmosphere for alliance negotiations with Japan.[5] When the Japanese approached him in June with a plan for a military alliance against Russia, Ribbentrop seized the opportunity to expand the projected anti-Soviet pact into an alliance which would apply against the Western powers as well. Several months of negotiations ensued—negotiations which eventually failed in the summer of 1939, primarily because Ribbentrop demanded, and the Japanese refused, an effective military pact against the Western powers.[6] But failure merely caused Ribbentrop to shelve, not to abandon, his idea; the plan to use Japanese naval power to "neutralize" a potential Western opponent of Germany was revived in August 1940—only this time it was aimed at the United States.

The record of the tedious German-Japanese negotiations of 1938–1939 suggests that the two powers viewed their projected alliance from very different angles. Germany insisted on a pact applicable against the West as well as against Russia; Japan was unwilling to go beyond an anti-Soviet alliance. In view of her economic dependence on Western markets and the caution of her naval leaders, she refused to risk a conflict with the Western powers. Germany desired an ironclad alliance that would bring Japan into the war automatically once Germany had been attacked. Japan wished to reserve greater freedom of action once the *casus foederis* arose.

The negotiations also disclose a German misunderstanding that persisted throughout World War Two: the German authorities failed to see how limited was Japan's war potential and how great were her aims.

Overestimating Japan's strength and underestimating her ambitions, Berlin time and again was to approach Japan with schemes which were neither militarily feasible nor politically attractive to the Japanese.

In contrast to Berlin, Tokyo in the late 1930s continued to view the German-Japanese rapprochement as primarily an anti-Russian alignment. For decades, events and Japan's interpretation of them had pointed to Russia as the major power with which her own imperialism might one day clash. The probability of a duel with the Soviet Union was never far from Japanese military minds in the 1930s, and Japan's signing of the anti-Comintern pact had reflected her need for an anti-Russian ally.

Japan's need for a European friend only grew as she acquired new opponents in 1937. Tokyo now hoped that German mediation or German pressure would make the Chinese yield to Japan's terms. When this hope faded by early 1938, Japan sought an outright military alliance with Germany against Russia, by then China's most effective ally. Such an alliance, the Japanese hoped, would deter Soviet intervention on behalf of China and might even cause the Soviets to abandon their aid to Chiang Kai-shek.[7]

Along with military considerations, two other durable components of the Japanese approach to Berlin had appeared by the late 1930s. Extremely sensitive in the matter of *de jure* recognition, Japan sought and by early 1938 obtained German recognition of Manchukuo.[8] Henceforth, Japan eagerly sought from Germany the recognition of the emergent New Order which no other great powers were willing to bestow. As time went on, mutual recognition of the

New Orders became one of the strongest links between Berlin and Tokyo.

Second, Japan came to look toward Germany as a potential major supplier of technical know-how and equipment, especially with reference to her various schemes for Manchurian development. As her economic relations with the Western industrial nations grew more precarious in the late 1930s, Japan began to look upon an alliance with Germany as part of a wider plan involving a complete economic reorientation that would render her largely immune to the pressures with which the Western powers hoped to stay her expansionist course in Asia.

By the late 1930s, Japan and Germany were associated, after a fashion, through a superficial resemblance of their ideologies and a convergence of their foreign political objectives: both wanted to establish and lead New Orders in their parts of the world, and both therefore threatened the peace and security of the powers, large and small, who were then rallying around the League of Nations and collective security. At the same time, German and Japanese timetables for expansion differed and the order in which they proposed to eliminate their enemies did not coincide. Risks of war with one or another potential opponent were weighed differently in Berlin and Tokyo; the two governments had not agreed on which third powers would have to be attacked, neutralized, or cut in on the spoils. These discrepancies, along with the two powers' propensity to take unilateral uncoordinated action (so marked a feature of their alliance after 1940), had begun to flaw German-Japanese cooperation before 1940. Two examples will suffice.

Japan's attack on China in 1937 came as a blow to the Germans. The Incident, as it soon came to be called, increasingly deprived Japan of that extra margin of strength which she needed to play the role that Germany had meant to assign to her. Yet Germany was unable to extricate Japan from her continental entanglement. German mediation did not settle the conflict, and the withdrawal of German military advisers from China in the spring of 1938, a significant pro-Nipponese gesture, did not lighten Japan's military burden.

By the same token, Hitler's unilateral moves in Europe in late 1938 and 1939 rendered coordination of policies with Japan more difficult. As Hitler accelerated his timetable for expansion by first setting aside the Munich settlement and then threatening Poland, the risk of Germany's finding herself at war with France and Britain mounted. Under these circumstances, Japan's refusal to conclude an unconditional alliance with Germany against Britain and France only became more stubborn. By the summer of 1939, Germany had abandoned any serious effort to paralyze Britain by a German-Japanese alliance and turned instead to a pact with the Soviet Union. By signing the Russo-German Pact on August 23, 1939, when Japanese negotiators in Berlin were still pursuing an anti-Soviet alliance, Germany added insult to injury. The news of the pact caused as much shock in Tokyo as in London, so much that the pro-German cabinet of Count Kiichiro Hiranuma fell.

WINTER OF THEIR DISCONTENT

Germany's about-face, at the very time when Japanese troops were engaged in undeclared border warfare with Soviet units in Siberia, froze German-Japanese relations for the next six months. Though the German leaders blandly assured Japan that Berlin wanted to be friends with both Moscow and Tokyo,[9] Japan turned for the time being to relatively pro-Western and anti-German cabinets. In many Japanese circles Germany's "treachery" had shattered trust in German candor and reliability for years to come.

The outbreak of the Second World War found Japan parading a neutrality distinctly unfriendly to Germany—or so the Germans thought. Throughout the early months of World War Two the Japanese complied with British blockade measures and refused to help Germany significantly in the purchase of strategic raw materials in Asia and the Americas.[10] To some German diplomats it even appeared that Japan might ultimately join the Western camp. When the Chinese government approached Berlin that winter with a new request for mediation in the China Incident, the German Foreign Ministry declined, for once satisfied that Japan should continue to be tied down on the Asiatic continent. It reasoned:

> The preliminary question is whether at the present time it is in the interest of Germany to bring about peace between China and Japan. As long as there was hope of getting Japan to conclude an alliance with Germany, the question could be answered in the affirmative without further ado. There was then an immediate possibility that, after the adjustment with the Soviet Union which we sought, Japan would turn resolutely against England. The present attitude of Japan does not indicate that this objective will be attained in the near future. As things stand today there is no very clear danger, to be sure, but nevertheless there is a possibility that in the course of a long German-British-

French war Japan might also line up on the other side. From this viewpoint, it would be to our interests for Japan to continue to tie up her forces in China.[11]

If the German diplomats had cause to complain against Japan, the Japanese government also fretted. The outbreak of the war in Europe had failed to provide Japan with that grand opportunity to enhance her power in Asia which she had enjoyed in 1914. During the crisis of August 1939 and the early months of the war, only Britain felt constrained by the events in Europe to make a few concessions which fortified Japanese control in North China.[12] Russia, neutral in Europe and protected by her pact with Hitler and Germany's military engagements elsewhere, was under no pressure to yield to Japan. On the contrary, by the middle of September she was able to negotiate an advantageous settlement of her border skirmishes with Japan after military successes had paved the way.

Between September 1939 and May 1940, Germany and Japan went their separate ways, both pursuing wars that had not yet merged into one. What caused their separate paths once more to converge were the German victories over Holland, Belgium, and France in the early summer of 1940. It was these victories, and the effect they produced in Japan, which formed the immediate background to the conclusion of the Tripartite Pact.

THE COURTSHIP RESUMED

To many Japanese the victories seemed to herald a shift in the world balance of power. A new division of colonial empires was at hand, they believed, and only a rapprochement with the victor would permit Japan to move into the power vacuum left in Southeast Asia in the wake of the German victories. In June and July 1940, the initiative for closer German-Japanese relations came from Tokyo, not Berlin.

During these two months the Japanese naval and general staffs, as well as senior officials in the foreign ministry, mapped out the details of a new rapprochement with Germany. Both military and civilians laid major stress on a mutual recognition of the New Orders as a fundamental principle of a tripartite alignment. The desire for German recognition of Japanese hegemony in Southeast Asia reflected Japanese fears that Germany herself might appropriate the Asiatic colonies of Holland and France. Another element in the drafts by both military and civilian officials was the hope for German mediation of outstanding Russo-Japanese problems. Japan, in other words, had come around to the logic expressed by Ribbentrop the previous fall, when he had declared that the German-Soviet pact might in the end benefit Japan. Oblivious of such recent symptoms of German-Soviet friction as the tension over the Baltic states or the Bukovina, the Japanese rather naïvely assumed that Germany's paramount position on the continent and her cordial relations with Russia would bring about a Soviet-Japanese *détente,* chiefly at the expense of Soviet interests.[13] An outright military alliance with Germany was not envisaged at this stage of the deliberations.[14]

The incumbent Yonai government, while preparing in this fashion the new rapprochement with the Rome-Berlin Axis, had fallen behind the tempo of the times. While civil servants weighed drafts of a tripartite agreement, the clamor of press and public opinion for a more aggressive government and the inability of the cabinet to make any headway in its approaches to Berlin led by mid-July to the overthrow of the government. Engineered by strongly pro-Axis elements in the army, the government crisis installed in the seats of power a new group of leaders whose domestic and foreign record was designed to inspire confidence not only among Japanese expansionists but also in Germany.

The new cabinet, with Prince Fumimaro Konoye at the helm, Yosuke Matsuoka in the foreign ministry, and Hideki Tojo in the army ministry, amalgamated the foreign ministry's and the services' drafts for a German-Japanese rapprochement and began negotiations with Germany on August 1, 1940. While the cabinet as a whole had not yet sanctioned the idea of a formal military alliance with Germany, Foreign Minister Matsuoka agreed in principle to Japanese military cooperation in the war against Britain. Vis-à-vis the United States, however, even the foreign minister sanctioned nothing more daring than a clause on German-Japanese consultation in case either got involved in hostilities with America.[15]

It was fortunate for the Japanese that, just as the new cabinet embarked on formal negotiations, Germany too was beginning to give more serious thought to a rapprochement with Japan. The Germans were ready to respond to Japanese overtures not only because Matsuoka spoke for a more aggressive cabinet, but because their own strategic predicament sent them once more in search of a Far Eastern ally.[16]

Until the middle of July, Hitler had expected that his victories on the continent would suffice to make England ready for peace. Indeed, he seems to have been anxious to conclude peace, or at any rate a truce, which would leave him the supremacy of continental Europe and a free hand toward the east and which would leave the British the empire. Under these circumstances, closer ties with Japan seemed unnecessary, even undesirable. Hitler is known to have referred contemptuously to the Japanese as "harvest helpers"[17] when they sought closer ties with Germany in June and early July, and many Germans feared that a rapprochement with the Japanese, at this juncture, could only complicate the peace settlement with Britain.

During the second half of July, however, it became apparent to Hitler that Great Britain had no intention of dealing with him on his own or any terms. His whole concept of the future conduct of the war and his attitude toward the remaining neutrals changed accordingly. For one thing, preparations for a cross-channel invasion of the British Isles, ordered in early July, were pushed forward by the services during the remainder of that month and throughout August. Almost as soon as preparations had begun, however, the military difficulty of such a hastily conceived scheme, compounded by the inability of army and navy to agree on operational details, impressed itself on Hitler. Afraid of losing prestige if the invasion miscarried, he soon began to cast about for an alternative strategy to bring Britain to terms.

For some time Hitler's attention turned to a "peripheral" strategy involving a series of attacks on vulnerable outposts of the British Empire. General Alfred Jodl, chief of staff of OKW (Supreme Command of the Armed Forces), had in late June advocated such operations in addition to an invasion of Britain herself. In this connection, Jodl had explained that "the fight against the English empire can only be conducted through or with the help of countries who are interested in the collapse of the English empire and hope for a substantial inheritance. These are primarily Italy, Spain, Russia and Japan. To cause these states to act is the task of diplomacy."[18]

The German navy vigorously supported this plan, and German diplomats pursued it in Madrid and even in Vichy during the fall of 1940. Hitler himself eventually tried to win France to a policy of collaboration and Spain to an entry into the war, but no attempt was made in the summer and fall of 1940 to bring the Japanese into the war against Britain.

In fact, by the end of July, Hitler had developed an absorbing interest in other plans. He had become convinced that Britain stubbornly refused to come to terms out of two hopes: that Russia could be detached from the anti-British bloc, and that the United States would eventually rally to Britain's support, at least with measures short of war. The diary of General Franz Halder, chief of staff of OKH (Supreme Command of the Army), provides vivid and detailed evidence of the anxiety felt on both scores by Hitler and his generals in late July and August. To meet the situation, it was necessary above all, Hitler thought, to clarify Germany's relations with the Soviet Union, already troubled of late by the Russian absorption of the Baltic states and the northern Bukovina. Such a clarification might be achieved by war—an alternative Hitler seriously considered in the last days of July—or by negotiations which would commit the Soviet Union unmistakably to the German cause. Whichever course Hitler chose—from August to November a diplomatic solution was sought and preparations for a campaign in 1941 were also begun—it was bound to affect Germany's relation with Japan. Hitler's views were paraphrased by Halder on July 31:

> *England's hope is Russia and America. If hope in Russia is eliminated, America too is eliminated,* because elimination of Russia means a tremendous increase of Japan's power in East Asia. *Russia is England's and America's sword against Japan in East Asia.*[19]

In search of its own Far Eastern "sword," the German government in August decided to seek a military alliance with Japan in order to intimidate the United States into continued neutrality in the German-British war. This seemed all the more necessary when the United States, during August and September, gave evidence of her confidence in Britain's ultimate survival and her support of the British cause.[20]

Despite the seeming convergence of German and Japanese goals, the negotiations begun by Matsuoka on August 1 made little progress. By the middle of the month Berlin decided to send a special emissary to Tokyo to discover Japan's intentions and to aid the ambassador in treaty negotiations. While the emissary, Minister Heinrich Stahmer, was en route to the Far East (August 23 to September 7), the conversations in Tokyo continued to languish as the Japanese cabinet held further sessions to map out the maximum offer that Nippon might make to the German negotiating team. Like its predecessor, the Konoye cabinet considered mutual recognition of spheres and German good offices in Moscow as the primary Japanese desiderata. The really difficult issue for Japan was whether she should commit herself to a forthright, automatic military alliance with Germany against all comers.[21]

It is important to realize just what the Japanese cabinet had decided by the time the German special envoy arrived. While a pro-German political alignment was generally favored, the exact terms of a military alliance—which Germany was expected to demand—remained undecided. The navy minister held out against an anti-British alliance, though lower echelons in the navy were prepared to take a bolder course. The foreign ministry seemed to throw caution to the winds in its alliance draft of September 1, in which for the first time the United States was mentioned, alongside Britain, as a target of the alliance. But during the first week of September, the highest navy echelons still held out against an automatic commitment to Berlin, even after Navy Minister Zengo Yoshida had been replaced by Koshiro Oikawa on September 4. The danger therefore existed that the alliance negotiations, just like those of 1938–1939, might reach an impasse on the scope of the military alliance and the rigor with which it was to be applied.

In the event, the negotiations of 1940 led to a pact where those of 1938–1939 had failed. Minister Stahmer, a close confidant of Ribbentrop, began negotiations with Matsuoka on September 9, and a short eighteen days later a Tripartite Pact and several bilateral (German-Japanese) exchanges had been signed. (These are reproduced in Appendix One.) The explanation for the success of 1940 is remarkable and throws an unexpected light on the supposedly totalitarian quality of German diplomacy: while publicly Japan signed an anti-American treaty as the Germans wished, secretly she obtained a release from her treaty obligation. The waiver was issued by the German negotiators on their own responsibility, without the knowledge and against the instructions of the German foreign minister.[22]

A PACT FOR A SEASON

Statesmen and journalists commented at the time that the treaty had all the marks of a German diplomatic victory.[23] They referred in this context primarily to Article III of the published treaty, in which the signatories:

> undertake to assist one another with all political, economic and military means when one of the three Contracting Parties is attacked by a Power at present not involved in the European War or in the Sino-Japanese Conflict.

Read in the light of Article V, which exempted the Soviet Union from the provisions of the alliance, Article III seemed to give Germany what she desired most: a defensive military alliance against the United States. The treaty might indeed appear like a poor bargain for Japan, had it not been for the provisions of the first secret addendum. This secret letter modified the alliance obligation of Article III in two important ways: it deprived the alliance of its automatic character by leaving it to the three governments to decide if and when the *casus foederis* had occurred. It restored an automatic and unconditional obligation to render military assistance against the United States, but this time unilaterally, as a one-sided promise of support which Germany extended to Japan.

The importance of the secret addenda and the circumstances of their conclusion have not been fully appreciated in the literature on the Tripartite Pact. The value to Japan of the secret annexes is clear from Matsuoka's refusal to conclude the pact without the accompanying secret understanding. The Japanese navy simply would not have given its assent to the alliance without the secret release.[24] Other groups in the Japanese ruling circle were won over to the alliance by one or another of the secret provisions. The German government, far from sanctioning the secret provisions, resisted them stoutly to the end, just as it had opposed similar Japanese proposals through the spring of 1939. Had it not been for the high-handed behavior of the German diplomats in Tokyo, the Tripartite Pact negotiations of 1940 would most likely have shared the fate of the abortive negotiations of 1938–1939.

This point is emphasized, not to embarrass the German ex-ambassador or to cast the German negotiators in the role of innocent victims of Japanese cunning, but because without such emphasis a true appreciation of the German-Japanese entente of September 1940 and its history in subsequent months is impossible. From the start, the German and Japanese governments had different conceptions of what the alliance offered and demanded; nor did time remove the initial misunderstanding. The German government never learned of the secret addenda to the pact, nor did the Japanese realize that the German Foreign Minister did not stand behind the assurances of his representatives.[25]

The full meaning of the pact can be grasped at two levels: at a somewhat legalistic level, by weighing the contractual obligations of each side against those of the other and against the objectives pursued; and at a more practical level, by examining the actual value of the alliance to each partner over a period of time.

From the juridical point of view, Japan appeared to have the advantage. On paper, she had realized her three most important objectives: German recognition of her unqualified political and economic hegemony in East and Southeast Asia; a German promise to work through Moscow for the improvement of Japanese-Russian relations; and a German promise of technical assistance in the further development of Japan's war industry. Further, she had won benefits not even particularly anticipated in the deliberations of her ministers: a unilateral promise of German military help in a war with the United States; a more vaguely worded German promise of aid in a British-Japanese war; and a settlement, to Japan's benefit, of the question of the former German colonies in the Pacific. The price Japan paid for these gains was relatively small: recognition of the German-Italian sphere in Europe, and, in the face of the world, a promise to come to the aid of Germany should the latter be attacked by the United States. While she was, as we have seen, absolved from a strict interpretation of this latter clause by virtue of the secret annexes, the promise still cost her something, for she would have to expect adverse reaction to it, particularly in the United States and Britain.

The German side of the ledger looked different. Germany's main objective, the iron-clad military alliance against the United States, had eluded her. Even if the pact was expected to prove its value primarily in the German war of nerves against the United States, not in the "hot war" which Hitler was determined to avoid for many more months to come, the secret provisions were embarrassing. To paralyze the United States with a German-Japanese alliance was difficult at best; to expect to intimidate her with a pact whose bluff might be called any day was self-defeating.

For this emasculated alliance Germany paid a substantial price. For one, she recognized Japan's New Order in Greater East Asia. While this seems evenly balanced at first glance by Japanese recognition of the German New Order, Germany had vastly more to lose in East and Southeast Asia than Japan in Europe or Africa.[26] Germany's attempts to salvage something—a special status for German business in East Asia, to be written into the secret annexes—failed again. In addition, Germany gave the Japanese one-sided guarantees of military assistance and surrendered a claim to the former German islands which might have been used as a bargaining point at some other time.

While the sum total of contractual obligations made the pact a diplomatic victory for Matsuoka, its actual implementation proved disappointing for both partners. For Japan, the German recognition of Greater East Asia remained without much real value as long as the Western powers withheld their sanction. Moreover, Germany soon began to compete with Japan for the raw materials of Indo-China, which clearly belonged to Japan's New Order. Above all, Germany's failure to bring the war against Britain to a victorious conclusion began to vitiate the alliance in Japanese eyes. Ironically, as we now know, during the very days when the Tripartite Pact was being negotiated, the tide had turned in the battle of Britain,[27] exposing the fateful limits of Hitler's continental victories.

Japan believed that the ally she had sought during the summer of 1940 and found by September was a Germany victorious on the continent of Europe and intimately allied to the Soviet Union. In fact, Germany was neither one by August–September 1940; otherwise she would not have troubled to conclude the pact with Japan. Only gradually did it dawn on the Japanese how mistaken their assumptions had been. By November it must have been clear to them, for instance, that German good offices in Moscow had brought no Russian concessions on the points at issue between Japan and the Soviet Union. During his visit to Berlin in November, Foreign Minister Vyacheslav Molotov explained that Russia would not recognize the Japanese New Order as currently defined in Tokyo, and he declared quite specifically that a Soviet-Japanese rapprochement would not be possible at the expense of the Chinese.[28] For a neutrality pact or nonaggression pact with Moscow, Molotov insisted, the Japanese would have to pay, not be paid. Molotov's price—the surrender of Japan's concessions in Northern Sakhalin and of her ambition to dominate China—left little doubt that the Germans were ineffective, if honest, brokers on Japan's behalf.

When Matsuoka perceived that a Soviet-Japanese rapprochement was not likely to be achieved via Berlin, he once more reverted to direct Russian-Japanese negotiations, which had, indeed, never been broken off. Though he later denied it, he now quite consciously used the growth of German-Soviet tension in the Balkans to gain his objective. By playing on Soviet fears of a two-front war, he hoped to gain Soviet consent to Japan's New Order in return for a nonaggression pact which would also free Japan's rear in case of further ventures in the south. Just how openly Matsuoka played this card through his ambassador in Moscow or during his own stay in the Soviet capital in late March and again in April 1941 is hard to tell. But there is little doubt about his intention, to judge from the statement he made to the Privy Council on December 18, 1940, on the occasion of the accession of Slovakia, Hungary, and Rumania to the Tripartite Pact. Said Matsuoka, in the awkward translation of the Tokyo Tribunal:

> This empire ought to agree to the enhancement to any extent of Germany's position in the Balkan peninsula, for one of the objectives of the Three-Power Alliance lies in taking advantage of the alliance in order to adjust Russo-Japanese relations. . . . I deem it a good policy to aggrandize the German menace to Soviet Russia availing ourselves of the situation to regulate our relations with Soviet Russia, seeing that Soviet Russia does not find any menace in Japan and is inclined to reject the adjustment of Russo-Japanese relations.[29]

In the end, the Japanese themselves achieved the desired protection in the north which Germany had been expected to secure for them. Bilateral Russo-Japanese negotiations and the personal intervention of Matsuoka in Moscow led to the conclusion of a neutrality pact with the Soviet Union on April 13, 1941.[30] Even so, Japan had to pay a price (the eventual return to Russia of her concessions in Northern Sakhalin) and the neutrality pact was considered less valuable than the nonaggression pact which had been Japan's original goal.

Other hopes which Japan had entertained at the time of her pro-Axis diplomatic realignment in 1940 remained unfulfilled by the spring of 1941. Her consolidation of Greater East Asia had made no progress and the expected economic and technical aid from the Reich had not arrived.

Germany had found the pact equally barren. It had not significantly neutralized the United States, nor did it prevent the Roosevelt administration from extending further aid to Great Britain. If anything, the conclusion of the Tripartite Pact probably alerted American public opinion to a sense of danger and created an atmosphere in which the President could proceed cautiously to align his nation more closely with the British. After a period of restraint imposed by the needs of the American presidential campaign, the newly re-elected President clearly indicated America's stand, especially in his "arsenal of democracy" speech of December 29, 1940. As soon as the new Congress assembled, the President introduced the lend-lease legislation; it had passed by March 1941.

Similarly, American military planners did not react to the Tripartite Pact in the manner anticipated by the Germans. They had already proceeded for some time on the assumption that America might be faced by simultaneous attacks from Japan and Germany. The Tripartite Pact merely confirmed that assumption. Hitler's hope that the pact would produce a shift in American strategic planning from an Atlantic to a Pacific orientation proved vain. On the contrary, the pact's military clause worked, if anything, to the advantage of Japan. It strengthened the sentiment among American military planners to remain on the defensive in the Pacific, paying political concessions if need be, in order to keep the United States free to aid Britain if that should become necessary.[31]

NEW WINE IN OLD BOTTLES

For both Japan and Germany, the Tripartite Pact had proved a grievous disappointment before the end of its first six months. As if the pact were a lamp that needed only to be rubbed in the right way to bring out its power, the Germans then tried to turn it into something it had never been: an offensive military alliance against Great Britain. Germany's re-examination of her relation to Japan again followed, as in the previous summer, on evidence of Britain's remarkable staying power during the winter of 1940–1941. The British had mounted an offensive in Africa during the winter and had inflicted heavy losses on the Italians, forcing Hitler to send German units to his ally. Re-examining Japan's role in the German war effort, the Germans soon found a panacea for most of their frustrations in the idea of an immediate Japanese entry into the war against Britain, a suggestion that had been brushed aside when the Japanese had raised it as a matter of information in September 1940.

The attempt to induce Japan to attack Singapore dominated German diplomatic efforts vis-à-vis Japan during the first half of 1941. Although the assumptions underlying this attempt are well known, the precise source of the project is uncertain. Possibly, the idea originated at the same time with the German navy in Berlin and the embassy in Tokyo.[32] The German navy, at any rate, soon became the most insistent sponsor of the project, which fitted in well with the navy's "peripheral" strategy against Britain. The navy, engaged in a final attempt to dissuade Hitler from his projected invasion of Russia, seized on the Singapore plan combined with a German-Italian attack on the Middle East as a substitute for the attack on Russia.

While the German naval high command was most anxious to see the Japanese attack Britain, it was also more aware than the other services of the risk of such an attack. In a long memorandum of February 4, 1941,[33] the navy weighed the advantages of a Japanese attack on Singapore against the danger of

American entry into the war. The navy concluded that, for Germany, the risk was worth taking; if the United States entered the war in the wake of Japan's attack on Singapore, American aid to Britain would be curtailed and the American war effort would be shifted from the Atlantic to the Pacific. Furthermore, the German navy claimed, Japanese attacks on British shipping would be even more beneficial to Germany than the attack on Singapore, since Britain's naval forces would then have to be even further dispersed. The navy recommended that Germany and Japan establish a "combined staff" or "supreme war council."

Hitler was sufficiently impressed by the navy's arguments to authorize a careful study of the possibilities of German-Japanese military collaboration. As a result of these investigations, a directive on "Collaboration with Japan" was issued by OKW on March 5. It reads in part:

> It must be the aim of the cooperation based on the Tripartite Pact to cause Japan to take action in the Far East at the earliest opportunity. Strong English forces will thus be tied down, and the focus of American interests will be diverted to the Pacific. In view of the still undeveloped preparedness for war of her enemies, Japan will have the greater chance of success the earlier she strikes. The "Barbarossa" operation [German invasion of Russia] will create especially favorable political and military preconditions for her.[34]

Even before the directive had been issued, Ribbentrop had set to work to win the Japanese over to this new plan,[35] but a puzzling contradiction in the German position tied his hands. While the attack on Russia was supposed to furnish Japan with the golden opportunity to strike at the south, all German authorities were strictly forbidden by the OKW directive to inform the Japanese of the forthcoming campaign. Furthermore, the Germans could never quite make up their minds which way to argue: that the Japanese attack on Singapore would increase the risk of an American entry into the war against Japan or that it would reduce that risk. The original German navy memorandum had held that there was a distinct risk but that it was worth taking. Even Hitler seems to have shared this view.[36] Yet in his conversations with the Japanese and in his instructions to Ambassador Ott, Ribbentrop never admitted that there was such a risk. He was therefore unable to quiet the fears of the more cautious Japanese officers, who felt sure that an attack on Singapore would bring the United States into the war. On the contrary, Ribbentrop always argued that only a Japanese attack on Britain could guarantee continued American neutrality.

German efforts on behalf of the Singapore project remained fruitless and had probably been doomed from the start. The Germans did not see this clearly for some time, because they misinterpreted Japan's proposals for joint operational plans (probably presented to Berlin in the hope of obtaining technical aid) as evidence of her readiness to strike.[37] Unlike Ribbentrop, the Japanese services always assumed that a strike against Britain would bring the United States into the war; at least down to June 1941 they thought that Japan could not take on such a formidable coalition. In fact, at the very time when the German directive on cooperation with Japan was being drafted, the Japanese navy vetoed an army plan for an attack on Malaya and the Dutch East Indies, precisely because it thought that war with England would draw the United States into the conflict.[38] The

German effort to convert the Tripartite Pact from a defensive alliance against the United States into an offensive alliance against Britain had failed before it was even officially launched.

Foreign Minister Matsuoka's visit to Europe in March and April 1941 reflected the disarray that had come to mark the German-Japanese alliance within six months after its conclusion, yet the visit did little or nothing to repair the damage. In Moscow, as we have seen, Matsuoka finally secured a pact, not because of German good offices, but because the growing German threat against the Soviet Union had persuaded Stalin that a neutrality pact with Japan was timely. Warned by his German hosts against intimate dealings with Moscow, Matsuoka angered his allies by concluding the neutrality pact. At the same time, the Japanese Foreign Minister was not able to learn much in Berlin about future German moves. Whatever he may have gathered from hints and gossip about mounting German-Soviet tension, he was not officially notified about his ally's plans for an invasion of Russia; Hitler's failure once more to inform the Japanese in good time of a major decision caused the Japanese to lose face when the German attack on Russia did take place in June. On the German side, there was similar frustration, since Matsuoka did not give a concrete commitment to a Japanese attack on Singapore. After his return to Japan, it soon became evident in Berlin that Matsuoka's vague promises in this matter had meant little. A beautifully stage-managed demonstration of solidarity, the Matsuoka visit barely hid the contradictions in the alliance. Not only cooperation but even candid disclosure of future plans was absent on both sides.[39] The disarray in the alliance increased in the months after Matsuoka's visit to Europe. Independent, unilateral moves by the two allies, in both war and diplomacy, had shattered their common front by the fall of 1941.

TWO BLOWS AGAINST UNITY

The first of the new blows to the alliance was dealt by Germany. Her attack on the Soviet Union struck the Japanese as another instance of German perfidy; again, Tokyo had been only insufficiently informed of a momentous decision which affected relations between the two countries as profoundly as had Hitler's earlier about-face in August 1939. Prime Minister Konoye in fact considered the German attack on Russia as a violation of the Tripartite Pact and was henceforth inclined to feel absolved from the other provisions of the alliance, particularly those relating to the United States.[40] While few Japanese went as far as the premier, all realized that the German-Soviet conflict had made the coordination of German and Japanese plans infinitely more complicated at a time when Japan's own military designs were veering southward and sharpening her antagonism to America and Britain.

The German attack on Russia brought other Japanese objectives to nought. Japan's requests for technical aid from Germany, which Matsuoka had personally pressed in Berlin in April, would now have to be curtailed. Germany's own increased demands would fully absorb the industrial capacity from which Japan had hoped to profit. Besides, the last route over which shipments of some magnitude could be exchanged between the allies was now cut off.

Germany's failure to inform Japan in time of her preparations for war against Russia made it almost certain that Japan would not join her in an attack on the Soviet Union. Had the Germans informed Tokyo early in the spring, when Japan still had some room to maneuver, Japan might have committed herself to an attack on Siberia. Instead, Japan had proceeded with her own plans for expansion to the south; now she refused to attack the Soviet Union when Ribbentrop abruptly made the request in late June.

During July Japan merely reinforced the Kwantung army, in preparation for entering the war if Russia should collapse in the near future. But by early August the Japanese had already concluded that an attack on Siberia in 1941 was out of the question; the build-up of forces in Manchuria was discontinued and then reversed in favor of southern operations. In October Japan informed her ally that she would strike only if and when German troops reached the Volga.[41]

During the summer, while their own hopes of immediate victory still ran high, German leaders did not regret Japan's refusal to come into the war. In fact, many of them had considered Ribbentrop's request to the Japanese unwise.[42] By autumn, however, the military expressed disappointment and annoyance that Japan's presence in Manchuria did not tie down all of Russia's Siberian forces. And as the German-Soviet conflict continued, the Germans complained that Japan had failed in her duty to Berlin by not interrupting lend-lease shipments to Vladivostok.[43]

Germany had needlessly offended Japan, first by her secrecy, and then by her brusque demand that Japan fall in line with the new turn of events. German ineptness in this case once more demonstrated that Berlin had failed to take into account Japan's own ambitions for expansion and empire. These ambitions had by mid-1941 given a new dimension to Japanese expansion and had made it vastly more difficult for Japan and Germany to agree on joint policies. Ironically, the same Japanese push for mastery of Southeast Asia which in September 1940 had driven her into the German camp now led her to new courses of action detrimental to Germany's designs. The crucial Japanese act was her decision to penetrate farther into Southeast Asia even while the China Incident had not been brought to a close.[44]

The China Incident was no closer to a settlement in early 1941 than it had been six months earlier when Japanese military planners had first sketched the outline of Japan's ambitions in the south. Russia had not abandoned her aid to Chiang Kai-shek or consented to Japan's domination of China, though after June 1941 Soviet aid to Chungking was perforce reduced to a trickle. Japanese hopes of a negotiated peace with Chiang had dimmed, since neither military pressure nor the establishment and recognition by Japan of a puppet regime in Nanking in November 1940 had had a visible effect on the leader of Free China. Washington gave no promise of consenting, much less contributing, to Japanese hegemony in China, on which Japan continued to insist despite her reduced ability to achieve it.

Though victory in China eluded her, Japan in late 1940 and early 1941 began to contemplate new moves toward the south. She had already established her control over the northern part of French Indo-China in September 1940, primarily in order to gain access to raw materials and to tighten the blockade against Chungking. By December 1940, the Japanese military began to draw up plans for an advance into southern Indo-China in order to have it available as a springboard for possible action against Britain and the Dutch East Indies. For some months, the foreign minister was able to stave off the services' requests that he secure bases in southern Indo-China and a military alliance with Thailand. Matsuoka believed that the United States would not stand idly by while Japan swallowed the rest of Indo-China, and he insisted that the country must be prepared for a war with the Americans before she ventured farther into the French colony. The services refusing to give assurances of such readiness, the matter rested here during the early months of 1941.

By June, Matsuoka found it increasingly difficult to resist the pressure of the military for the proposed take-over of southern Indo-China. This move was now put forth as part of a broader scheme for Japanese expansion into Malaya and the Dutch East Indies. Negotiations with the Dutch about oil had broken down and the military insisted that the springboard for military action in the south be available before the monsoon season started. This meant that the demands on France would have to be presented in July at the latest. Since Matsuoka still insisted that Indo-China could not be considered in isolation, apart from the question of war or peace with the Western powers, the services in late June gave it as their opinion that the Indo-China action should be undertaken, even at the risk of war with the great naval powers. The decision was made lightly, almost casually, and chiefly to silence the obnoxious quibbles of the foreign minister; an imperial conference on July 2 confirmed the decision of the services. The possibility of Anglo-American sanctions short of war and how Japan might counter them was not seriously considered.

It is hard to understand the reasons for this remarkable and unusual irresponsibility on the part of the Japanese naval and general staffs. Perhaps the German attack on the Soviet Union, which guaranteed safety in the north, emboldened the services to run a risk which they had been unwilling to take earlier. Perhaps their specious distinction between "warlike" and "peaceful" penetration (Indo-China was to be a case of the latter) led them to underestimate the vigor of the Western response. Thus they were unprepared when the United States, Britain, and the Netherlands answered Japan's advance into southern Indo-China in late July with a total embargo of all deliveries to Japan.[45]

The embargo confronted Japan with stark alternatives, none of which fitted in with German plans. She could either abandon her plans for Greater East Asia for lack of sufficient resources to create the New Order by force, or she could use force to seize the oil of the Indies, bringing Britain and possibly the United States into the war. Even outright defiance by a direct attack on the United States was beginning to appeal to some naval circles in Tokyo. Both of these courses of action ran wholly counter to German designs. Down to late November it was not in Hitler's plans to be drawn into a conflict with the United States, either directly or by the back door of Asia. A third alternative, a partial retreat and a thorough negotiation of outstanding issues with the United States so as to get embargoes rescinded, was even more detrimental to Germany's designs in 1941. Yet it was precisely such a policy which Japan had adopted even before the embargo of late July made it seem to some the only alternative to war.

TOWARD A PACIFIC DETENTE

In April 1941 diplomatic talks between Tokyo and Washington had begun in the American capital; they struck Germany as an outright betrayal of the Tripartite Pact. The Hull-Nomura talks involved a searching and systematic examination of all the issues which had plagued Japanese-American relations during the last decade: the creation of Manchukuo, abridgment of American treaty rights in China, the China Incident, Japan's alliance with Hitler, and her threats to the *status quo* in Southeast Asia.[46]

A few Japanese and some Americans saw in these talks the last best chance for a Japanese understanding with the West, a reversal of her ten-year course of aggression, the resumption of normal trade relations, and the reassertion of the more peaceful elements in the Japanese body politic. The majority of American policy-makers held no such sanguine views but continued negotiations in the hope that they might at least prolong the truce in the Pacific which the service chiefs considered so important.

Their suspicions were well founded, since the Japanese course was shaped by men quite unprepared to make a basic reversal of policy. The Japanese leaders were willing, in the last analysis, to forgo expansion farther south (before July this meant expansion into southern Indo-China and places farther south) but they insisted that in return the Western powers must sanction Japanese control of Manchukuo and China.[47] In essence, then, the negotiations were a Japanese attempt to exploit America's unpreparedness and her preoccupation with Atlantic defense and aid to

Britain in order to consolidate and legalize the Japanese gains of the past decade.

When it became clear to the Japanese government (probably by May) that Washington refused to make these, or any, concessions, the once united front of the Japanese cabinet broke into splinters. Its members began to differ on the terms of a new offer to Washington, and some expressed doubts of the wisdom of negotiating at all. By mid-July disagreements over the conduct of negotiations had become so serious that Foreign Minister Matsuoka was forced to leave the cabinet, his departure giving a new lease on life to the party of negotiation.[48] Just when the departure of Matsuoka might have ushered in a more productive phase in the Washington talks, America's unexpectedly sharp reaction to the Japanese advance into southern Indo-China brought on a serious crisis in Japanese-American relations and a temporary halt to the talks. But the grave consequences of the oil embargo only made the grim Japanese choice between war or retrenchment more desperate; the Washington talks were reopened by August.

After the ouster of Matsuoka, one issue in Japanese-American negotiations seemed more amenable to solution. Matsuoka's successors were ready to meet the Americans more than halfway on the issue of their country's attitude toward the European war. Rejecting a formal renunciation of the Tripartite Pact, they nevertheless conveyed to the American government that Japan was not bound by Germany's interpretation of that treaty and that she reserved complete freedom of action. By fall the State Department showed marked gratification at the Japanese change of position in this respect.[49]

To Berlin, the Japanese-American negotiations of

1941 were clear proof of Germany's diplomatic failure and of her inability to keep the Tripartite alliance together even outwardly. When the German government had first heard of the Washington talks in early May, it insisted that the talks be used to reinforce the Tripartite Pact. As Ribbentrop explained to his Japanese colleague, the United States could be kept out of the war only by "the brutally frank demonstration that whatever America might do, and however she might motivate her actions or whatever the measures applied by her might be, her entrance into the war would in all circumstances compel Japan to intervene."[50]

The German government further demanded that it be kept informed of the progress of the talks and that it be shown the Japanese counterproposals before they were submitted to Washington.

The Japanese refused to accede to the German requests. For instance, Japanese proposals of May 12 were shown to Berlin only after they had been submitted in Washington. Further German requests to participate in the talks were likewise ignored; the American counterproposals of June 21 were not even shown to Berlin for about three weeks and the Japanese notes of mid-July were also shown to Berlin only after it was too late to modify them.[51]

Moreover, the substance of the Japanese proposals to Washington, as far as they concerned the Tripartite Pact, appeared quite inadequate to the Germans. Ambassador Ott informed the Japanese, for instance, that their note of May 12 struck him as "tantamount to a legalization of American interventionist policies [in the Atlantic war]," whereas Ribbentrop considered the note an "absolute minimum" only if accompanied by a firm Japanese declaration of loyalty to the Tripartite Pact and by American assurances not to enter the European war.[52] Needless to say, no such declaration or assurances were forthcoming. Nor did Japan break off the talks, as Germany had counseled when she realized that she would be unable to shape them.[53]

The Japanese-American conversations came at a particularly awkward time for Germany. During the spring of 1941, Berlin was afraid that the United States might become more deeply engaged on Britain's side in the Atlantic war. Hence, Germany did not want her Pacific ally to negotiate at Washington but to stand ready to intimidate the Americans into strict neutrality. Germany invoked the Tripartite Pact in May when she feared that the United States might institute convoy escorts any day. The Japanese were asked to declare in Washington that further American trailing of German vessels or the escorting of convoys would bring Japan into the war.[54] The obliging Matsuoka told the Germans that he had issued such a warning, but to the American ambassador he spoke differently. He explained that, in his personal estimation, Japan would have to stand by Germany were she attacked by further patrolling or by convoy escorts, implying that the cabinet did not share his views, as indeed it did not.[55] Only ignorance kept the Germans from crying perfidy. In the end, the May crisis subsided, as President Roosevelt decided against escorting convoys for the time being. He did so, incidentally, out of consideration of American public opinion, and not because of Matsuoka's oblique warning to Ambassador Grew.[56]

Other strains in German-Japanese relations followed. In early July, Berlin suspected that the American occupation of Iceland was in part the result of fresh Japanese guarantees of quiescence in the Pacific, but the suspicion seems to have passed soon.[57] In September a more disturbing crisis in Tripartite relations arose in connection with the American "shoot on sight" order. The day after Roosevelt had published the order, Ribbentrop proposed

> an unmistakable, new statement by the Japanese Government to the effect that any further act by Roosevelt on the road of aggression against the Axis Powers will inevitably lead to a state of war between Germany and Italy on the one hand and America on the other; and that this will call forth the case of the alliance [*casus foederis*] provided for in the Tripartite Pact and immediately lead to Japan's entry into such a war against America.[58]

In response, the Japanese drew up a note to Washington only late in the month and much milder in tone, and explained to the German ambassador that the note would be delivered in Washington at a suitable opportunity, not immediately, as Ribbentrop had wanted. By early October, Ott had to report that the note, even in its watered-down form, had still not been sent. The "warning" Japan conveyed to Ambassador Grew on October 15 was more reassuring to Washington than responsive to Berlin.[59]

Berlin had a two-fold cause for complaint after August 1941: not only did Japan fail to live up to her alliance obligations (as interpreted in Germany), she also kept her ally completely in the dark as far as the resumed Washington talks were concerned. If Berlin had been mildly dissatisfied with Matsuoka's handling of these talks, it became thoroughly annoyed with Matsuoka's successors, Teijiro Toyoda (July to October) and Shigenori Togo (after October). Annoyance would have turned to fury had

Berlin been aware of the whole truth—a scrapping of the Tripartite Pact so unmistakable as to win praise even from the usually skeptical American Secretary of State, Cordell Hull. Unlike Matsuoka, his successors were ready to sacrifice the alliance with Germany to a Japanese-American agreement on Far Eastern issues.[60]

By the autumn of 1941 German and Japanese policies toward the United States, chief target of the Tripartite Pact, were working completely at cross purposes. Germany demanded Japanese action only to intimidate the United States into neutrality, but Japan was pursuing negotiations which, if successful, would strengthen America's capability to aid Britain against Hitler. If the negotiations proved unsuccessful, Japan might plunge into a war with America, a conflict Hitler was determined to prevent. Similarly, the allies' policies toward Russia were in complete disarray, particularly when from October on Japan began to urge Berlin to seek a negotiated settlement, while Ribbentrop from time to time asked Japan to join the war against Russia. The Japanese seem to have felt this impasse more acutely and in the fall of 1941 they set out to try to restore focus to the alliance.

THE PACT REFURBISHED

Leaving the Pact's outer shell intact, the Japanese set about to transform the alliance into something it never yet had been: an offensive military pact against the United States and Britain. Differing from the anti-Western pact which the Germans sought in 1938–1939 in order to intimidate third powers into neutrality, the new Japanese proposal aimed at an alliance for the impending war against America and

Britain. In October it was unwelcome in Berlin, not only because it implied an outright challenge to the United States in the Pacific but also because, in order to give focus to the new concept, it would have required Germany to negotiate an early peace with the Soviet Union.

Japan's new conception of the Tripartite Pact reflected her own needs and her own appraisals of the world situation. Negotiations with the United States were going badly, and, as war became more likely, a concentration of all the forces of the Tripartite allies on Japan's primary enemies, the United States and Britain, seemed indicated. At the same time, Japan once again sensed more surely than Germany the limitations of the Tripartite powers' resources. Convinced that it would be foolish to fight Russia, Britain, and America at the same time, and aware that Germany's offensive in Russia was not going to be another *blitzkrieg*,[61] the Japanese in early October began to urge a "political solution" to the Russo-German conflict. They were anxious to restore overland communications with Europe now that economic ties with the rest of the world were seriously impaired. But chiefly they wanted Germany to abandon her heavy commitments in the east and to release her forces for action against Japan's probable common foes: the United States and Britain.

On October 4, War Minister Hideki Tojo and Army Chief of Staff Hajime Sugiyama approached the German ambassador with such a proposal.[62] The exact German reply is not recorded, but if the Japanese message reached Ribbentrop or Hitler, the reply most certainly was negative. The Japanese soundings had come just two days after the start of the German offensive against Moscow, and for another ten days or so the German leaders were to be very sanguine about their chances of success.[63] Despite their initial failure, the Japanese were determined to renew their pressure for a negotiated German-Soviet peace at an auspicious moment. Meanwhile, the imperial conference of November 5 formulated Japan's last offer to the United States, set a deadline for negotiations, and decided to approach Germany with a request for participation in the war against America, should Japan's last offer to Washington prove unacceptable.[64] In this fashion did the Tripartite Pact, never primarily designed by the Japanese as a military pact against the Western powers, assume in their plans the shape of an offensive wartime military alliance.

Although Germany had for many months urged the Japanese to avoid a conflict with the United States, by the middle of November 1941 Germany's own relations with America had so deteriorated that Berlin was now no longer averse to the new Japanese overture for joint action against America. Once more, developments quite outside the German-Japanese relationship—this time, developments in the undeclared American-German war in the Atlantic—were drawing Berlin and Tokyo together.

During the first ten months of 1941, Germany had sought to avoid open conflict with the United States, even while America's espousal of belligerency would have furnished the German government with a number of opportunities to go to war in self-defense. In late April, for example, American naval forces manning the patrol of the Pan-American neutrality zone were ordered to "trail" German vessels and to report their positions—a great advantage to the British navy, whose forces were thinly strung out. In early July

American troops began to garrison Iceland under an agreement with the local government, while American forces began to escort American convoys between the United States and Iceland. In July American lend-lease aid was extended to the Soviet Union, and in August Churchill and Roosevelt met for the Atlantic Conference; their chiefs of staff continued strategic talks begun earlier in the year in Washington. In early September, after an incident between a German submarine and the trailing American destroyer *Greer,* Roosevelt issued the "shoot on sight" order. Canadian, British, and other ships were henceforth also permitted to join United States-escorted convoys to Iceland, and the Pan-American patrol area was extended to within 300 miles of the British Isles. At the end of the month convoy escorts were provided within this extended zone.[65]

America had thus become a belligerent in the Atlantic war, yet Hitler had accepted these developments with unaccustomed meekness. What apparently caused Germany to reconsider her policy was a change in the American neutrality legislation, signed into law on November 17. From now on American merchantmen would be armed and might enter the "war zone" immediately surrounding the British Isles. While Hitler had for months refused to be provoked by the unneutral acts of the American government, he now decided that the time had passed when he must restrain his submarines for fear of incidents with American naval and merchant vessels. The chief pressure for a change in German policy came from the German navy. In a request to OKW, the Supreme Command of the German Navy reasoned on December 2:

After the change in the [American] neutrality law, the

> desire to avoid incidents would needs lead to a prohibition of attacks against American ships even in the original blockade area which corresponds to the American war zone as hitherto defined. In the conversation of the Fuehrer with the C-in-C, Navy, however, the Fuehrer stated that this was not at all his intention.[66]

The navy requested permission to attack without warning all American war and merchant ships in the original blockade area, to attack American convoys and naval and merchant vessels with dimmed lights outside that zone, to consider American goods subject to contraband, and to disregard the Pan-American safety zone. On December 8, after the news of the Japanese attack on Pearl Harbor had arrived in Berlin, the naval staff confirmed its request of December 2 to OKW, explaining that the desired new orders (which so carefully stopped short of war) "would suffice . . . as a final solution for proceeding against U.S. forces."[67] OKW, which must have examined various possible responses to Pearl Harbor and the stepped-up Atlantic conflict, issued the order on the same day.[68] While the new directive resulted from the changed requirements of Atlantic warfare, Ribbentrop made political hay with it, telling Ambassador Hiroshi Oshima on December 8 that the new rules for the German navy, a first response to Pearl Harbor, were a prelude to a declaration of war.[69] Whether Hitler had already decided on war may be questioned. The navy was under the impression that no formal declaration of war was contemplated in the near future,[70] and OKW would presumably not have issued a directive which it knew would be superseded within a day or two.

Yet, within three days, the directive of December 8 *was* superseded by a declaration of war. The change in policy is not easy to explain. Perhaps Hitler found it easier to take the final step which he had studiously avoided for so long because the directive of December 8 made an increasing number of American-German incidents, and therefore war itself, more likely. Hitler was also under considerable pressure from his Japanese ally to join in the war. Japanese pressure had been applied since mid-November through regular diplomatic channels; it had been couched in the form of a Japanese request that Germany enter a tripartite agreement not to make a separate peace with Britain or the United States. There is evidence that Hitler had acceded to the Japanese request—virtually a promise of a declaration of war in the case of an American-Japanese conflict—by December 5.[71] This makes it all the more puzzling why the directive of December 8, which so carefully stopped short of war, was ever issued, and why it was not held up in favor of a declaration of war once the news of Pearl Harbor had been received.

One explanation for this apparent vacillation in German policy between December 7 (the news of the Pearl Harbor strike was received in Germany in the evening, local time) and December 11 (when Hitler proclaimed his declaration of war to the Reichstag) may be found in Hitler's preoccupation with a crisis on the Russian front. Severe cold and an effective Russian counteroffensive before Moscow had brought the German advance to a standstill by the end of the first week in December and serious reversals seemed possible. We know that Hitler had his hands full with the problems of the Eastern front in the days just before and after Pearl Harbor.[72]

But it is also possible that Hitler did not feel bound by his assurances of early December to Japan. Once informed of the Pearl Harbor attack, he may have waited for some days to make out America's response before committing Germany to war against the United States. In these days he must have weighed the advantages to Germany of neutrality or participation in a Japanese-American war. In particular, he must have speculated about American strategic plans in such a war and wondered whether America's war with Japan might bring the long-desired end of American aid to Britain.

We have some indication of how the German leadership sized up American strategic plans in early December. On December 4 the *Chicago Tribune* and other isolationist papers had leaked information on American grand strategy to the public.[73] The leaked material was accepted as genuine by the German government, and it is most probable that this material was taken into account as Hitler shaped German policy in the week before December 11. We have, in any case, the German navy's evaluation of the leaked material, though unfortunately not Hitler's own. If he, along with the armed services, accepted the material at face value and therefore believed that prior to Pearl Harbor the American government had been preparing an expeditionary army for use in Europe in 1943, this information may well have confirmed his decision to give his navy a freer hand against American shipping. The news of the Pearl Harbor attack may have convinced Hitler, as it convinced the navy and some of the diplomats, that American strategy would now be completely reoriented in favor of a primary commitment of forces to the Pacific.[74] Such an estimate would explain why the order to the navy was issued on December 8, while a declaration of war was withheld. By refusing to declare war,

Germany would reinforce the very natural American tendency to strike first against the most flagrant aggressor. Germany might finally reap the advantage which the Tripartite Pact had been designed to secure but had failed to provide. If such was the German calculation, its fallacy became clear in the evening of December 9 (United States time). In a radio speech, President Roosevelt made plain that America considered Germany equally guilty with Japan for the Pearl Harbor attack and that a concentration of the American war effort in the Pacific at the expense of other theaters was not to be expected.[75]

Under these circumstances, it may well have appeared embarrassing to Hitler to fail to respond to Japan's pleas for a German declaration of war, pleas that were by now being publicly voiced in Tokyo.[76] We need not assume that fidelity to his pledged word motivated Hitler. The order already given to the navy brought Germany very close to the brink of war with the United States; a new series of incidents was likely. At the same time, Hitler's military advisers assumed that a concentration of the American war effort in the European theater at the expense of the Pacific was not to be expected.[77] With these military estimates in mind, the temptation to take a bold step when Japan had given evidence of such boldness and to rescue the fiction of a grand alliance acting in unison may well have proved too hard to resist.

THE LOSS OF STRATEGIC INITIATIVE

2

Following their separate courses of action, Germany and Japan declared war on the United States within three days of each other. With her attacks on Malaya and Hong-Kong, Japan joined Germany in the war against Great Britain. The Western powers suspected a joint plot behind these moves and anticipated a common strategy by the Tripartite powers. They had overestimated their enemies' capacity for joint action. In contrast to the British and Americans, the German and Japanese governments had devised neither a plan nor a machinery for strategic coordination by December 1941. No military talks had been held. Each government, to be sure, had separately given some thought to what both might be doing in a joint war. But in the absence of joint consultation, such thoughts bore little relationship to reality. The German concept of joint naval warfare, for example, elaborated in the navy's memorandum of February 4, 1941, was based entirely on German interests and concepts of naval warfare. It proved most inappropriate for the kind of war that Japan was planning to fight after the attack on Pearl Harbor. The German navy had maintained:

> It is vital that Japan should play her part in the common war aim of the signatories of the Tripartite Pact, which is to overthrow the Anglo-American coalition. It must be made absolutely clear that any *selfish* interests must for the present be subordinated to this common aim. . . . Japan has several strictly limited national aims in her sphere. She must be made to realize very definitely that, regardless of these aims, the primary war aim is to combat the supply lines of the Anglo-American powers. This will be the task of the Japanese Navy in the Pacific and in the Dutch East Indies area. On no account should primary importance be accorded to landings or to seizure of areas which in-

> volve tying down essential parts of the Japanese fleet permanently, unless the execution of such projects is essential to the main task. . . . Even though annihilating blows can hardly be struck at the American surface forces, and in any case are not the main task of the Japanese surface forces, the latter must strive to tie down the largest possible portion of the USA fleet in the Pacific and to wear it down by keeping it constantly on the move. This diversionary activity would have a decisive influence on warfare in European waters.[1]

Whatever the soundness of these principles, the Germans had made no attempt to get Japanese agreement to such a naval strategy before Pearl Harbor. Had they tried, their success most certainly would have been small, in view of the Japanese navy's determination to annihilate the American fleet (whether in Pearl Harbor, as ultimately decided, or in naval action in the western Pacific, as envisaged in all the earlier war plans)[2] and to occupy all of Southeast Asia. There is no evidence that other German services or OKW had given any thought to joint strategy or operations or had conferred with Japan on this matter.

In Japan, the matter of joint Tripartite strategy had received more attention, and the Japanese services had developed a plan in early November that established priorities while dividing responsibilities between the Tripartite powers. Specifically, the Japanese believed that only England could be defeated militarily and that America would have to be "deprived of her will to fight"—that is, forced into a negotiated settlement. It would be Germany's and Italy's task to take the necessary military measures against Britain in Europe and the Middle East, while Japan's contribution to the downfall of the British Empire would consist of political, propaganda, and military action in East and Southeast Asia. Military action to establish communications between the Tripartite powers via the Indian Ocean was also envisaged by the Japanese. America's spirit of resistance was to be worn down, the Japanese planned, by spurring Philippine independence under the aegis of Japan, by cutting American trade with Asia, and by dealing heavy naval blows in the Atlantic and Pacific. In this fashion, the Japanese planners thought, the Tripartite powers might "deprive America of her will to continue [the] war."[3]

Entitled "Basic Principles for Rapid Conclusion of War against the United States, England, Netherlands, and the Chungking Regime," the plan was both more modest and more ambitious than the German navy's memorandum. In contrast to the German plan, it assumed that only one of the common enemies, Great Britain, could be defeated militarily. The United States, Japan thought, would have to be pressured into a negotiated agreement. On the other hand, the Japanese went a good deal further than the Germans in suggesting concerted military operations aimed at a specific area—the Indian Ocean. Presumably, cooperation of all three allies and their individual services would have to be worked out under such a plan. But the Japanese, like the Germans, had not broached the subject to their allies prior to Pearl Harbor;[4] their plan, like the German navy's, promised to run into trouble because of the ally's independent and divergent war aim: in this case, German priority for the war against the Soviet Union.

BARRIERS TO COOPERATION: MEN AND SYSTEMS

Not only had Germany and Japan failed to work out even the most tentative joint strategy before December 1941, they also lacked the combined staff system to whom the drafting of strategic plans might now be entrusted. The only Tripartite bodies that existed had been established in December 1940, pursuant to Article IV of the Tripartite Pact. They consisted of a main committee in each capital, composed of the resident foreign minister and the other two allies' ambassadors, and of military and economic subcommittees in Berlin, Rome, and Tokyo. Their establishment had been due to Japanese pressure, since Tokyo hoped to use the committees as channels for the presentation of her requests for technical aid in Germany. While technical aid was soon discussed bilaterally between Berlin and Tokyo outside the Tripartite committees, the committees themselves played no important role in the relations of the three powers during 1941. Their meetings were infrequent and ceremonial, and the presence of Italian representatives, whose discretion both Berlin and Tokyo distrusted, made them unfit instruments for strategic coordination between Germany and Japan. Besides, the representatives on the military committees were poorly informed about their own nations' strategic plans, much less empowered to commit those nations to a joint plan of action.

Both the Japanese ambassador to Germany and the German ambassador to Japan increased the difficulty of cooperation as a result of personal leanings or constitutional position. Hiroshi Oshima was so pro-German that he did not speak with the actual voice of Japan. He was the scion of a military family which had developed sympathies for Germany in Meiji days. A professional officer, he had served in Berlin as military attaché in the early 1930s before rising to the rank of ambassador in 1938. At the time of the Russo-German pact, he stiffly defended Germany's action, refusing even to deliver his own government's protest note to the Reich. His uncritically pro-German stand and his personal diplomacy cost him the sympathy of the government that assumed office in September 1939. In October Oshima was recalled. Though he was returned to Berlin as ambassador in February 1941, his services to the cause of German-Japanese unity were distinctly limited. He was poorly informed by his own government on the progress of Japanese-American negotiations and had to watch helplessly as German-Japanese relations deteriorated in the second half of 1941. In his dispatches to Tokyo, he frequently seemed to champion German rather than Japanese interests.[5] His own ready assent to the Singapore plan and other German schemes only increased German frustration in the long run, when Berlin discovered that what Oshima promised Tokyo by no means delivered. After Pearl Harbor, Oshima was kept largely in ignorance of his country's military plans, of which, under the Japanese constitution, even the foreign minister, his superior, knew little. By 1943 Tokyo considered him hopelessly out of touch with the real situation in Japan and much too optimistic about Nazi prospects.[6] He helped neither Berlin nor Tokyo to form an adequate estimate of the other's remaining strength. The man who more than any other Japanese enjoyed Hitler's personal confidence was thus ill equipped to become the intermediary for effective strategic cooperation.

On the other hand, Ott, the German ambassador in Tokyo, earned by his conduct too little, not too much, confidence from his hosts. The Japanese distrust of Ambassador Ott had developed in late 1941 in connection with the Sorge affair. Richard Sorge was the Tokyo correspondent of one of Germany's finest papers, the *Frankfurter Zeitung*, a shrewd observer of things Japanese, and a close friend of Ott. He was also a Russian spy. Although the Japanese may not have believed that the ambassador had entrusted secret information to Sorge, they never recovered their confidence in Ott.[7] Since the ambassador had access to the cables filed by his attachés (who reported to their services by general embassy cipher), the Japanese services were loath to confide to the German attachés information which Ott might compromise.

Neither the Germans nor the Japanese took immediate measures to relieve this situation at the time of Sorge's arrest in October 1941. But in the summer of 1942, as the need for military collaboration was felt more acutely and Ott had not recovered the confidence of the Japanese services, the German navy urged the appointment of a "German Admiral Tokyo." In the pattern of German-Italian liaison arrangements, this official was to represent OKW directly at Imperial General Headquarters, using his own cable facilities. Bypassing the incriminated ambassador, the Germans felt, would make the Japanese services more frank and cooperative. But there was the rub—Ribbentrop insisted that this downgrading of his ambassador was intolerable and by November he had defeated the whole project. In the end, the attachés did receive separate cable facilities and Ott was replaced by Stahmer in early 1943, too late to have had much effect on the common conduct of the war.[8]

Personality difficulties and sheer distance explain to some extent why the two nations did not accomplish better coordination of their war efforts. But the nature of their regimes and the structure of their respective governments played an even larger part. Though much has been said about the similarity of their totalitarian regimes, the processes of military decision-making in Germany and Japan were so dissimilar as to preclude successful consultation and cooperation.

In Japan, a long tradition of service rivalry had led to the development of specific procedures by which the general staff (army) and the naval staff coordinated their policies. As the military element became ever more dominant in the Japanese body politic, the interservice liaison conference assumed a decisive role in diplomacy as well as strategy. The two service ministries and their respective general staffs conferred almost permanently at most levels. As a result, the army and the navy were thoroughly familiar with each other's positions, however little love might be lost between them. At the same time, no single effective agency (discounting the largely passive emperor) stood over and above the services. Imperial General Headquarters, despite its resounding title, was merely another name for the top echelons of the two services, in which were continued the feuds and accommodations begun at lower levels.[9]

In Germany, on the contrary, Hitler permitted little contact between the services or between their chiefs. He often conducted his conferences with his single service chiefs separately, usually reserving final decisions for himself and his supraservice staff, the

OKW. The latter, however, appropriately headed by the man whose nickname pointed to his servility (General Wilhelm Keitel, nicknamed "Lakeitel," a play on the German word for lackey), acted more and more as the mere instrument of the Führer's military intuition. As the war progressed, and particularly after the crisis on the Russian front in December 1941, the army general staff and an increasing number of theaters of war also came under the direct influence of Hitler's unsystematic and impulsive working habits.[10]

These different structures—Germany's single authority over and above the services, which indeed asserted itself increasingly at the expense of professional military advisers, and Japan's framework for close if not always harmonious interservice consultation and cooperation—could not be fitted together closely, and German-Japanese coordination of war efforts became exceedingly difficult. The personal bond of Hitler and Mussolini, so crucial in German-Italian coordination, had no counterpart. Japan, lacking a supraservice equivalent to OKW, could only arrange for liaison from service to service. As the single services accounted for less and less in the German command structure, service-to-service liaison between the allies, so congenial to the Japanese, turned out to be inadequate. Yet arrangements for liaison between the two Japanese services and OKW remained most inadequate during the war. During the first eight months of joint warfare, the Japanese service representatives were not once received at OKW for consultation.[11]

Since the German navy was most keenly interested in cooperation with Japan, what little coordination of war efforts took place was usually conducted between the German naval high command, speaking wishfully for itself or authoritatively for Hitler, and representatives of the Japanese navy in Berlin.[12] Even so, the result could hardly be called coordination; no permanent combined staff was set up and meetings between the naval officers of the two nations took place only about once or twice a month. Too often, moreover, these meetings were mere courtesy calls, with some mutual briefing added, not serious working sessions.

Whatever the inadequacy of German-Japanese war planning, the powers attempted to improve it in the new situation of December 1941. As if first to wipe away past differences with an ultimate commitment, the three powers on December 11 supplemented their 1940 alliance with an agreement not to conclude a separate peace or an armistice with any of their common enemies except with prior consultation and consent.[13] Japan, which had suggested the agreement in the first place, turned out to be the only signatory that did not break the pact. In addition to this document, Japan had presented the draft of a military agreement which would assign each power its share in the common war effort.

A BLUEPRINT FOR JOINT WARFARE

The draft was submitted at the meeting of the Tripartite committee in Berlin on December 15, 1941, and after some minor modifications suggested by the German side it was signed at Hitler's headquarters on January 18, 1942.[14] The agreement, which is reproduced in Appendix Two, turned out to be the high-water mark rather than the modest beginning of German-Japanese military coordination. It was woefully inadequate in itself, and several of its clauses already foreshadowed the unsatisfactory course of German-Japanese wartime cooperation in the years to come. First of all, the agreement separated or delimited the powers' respective military tasks and spheres of operation, rather than providing for their integration. It assigned to Japan the Pacific and the Indian Ocean, between the west coast of America and the 70th degree eastern longitude, with all the continents and islands therein, and on the continent of Asia the area east of about the 70th degree eastern longitude. The German-Italian sphere of operations comprised all the areas west of the degree line to the east coast of America (see the map on page 111). The dividing line was to be treated flexibly by the respective navies, but on the whole it was assumed that operations beyond the assigned sphere would be rare and would be announced beforehand.[15]

Provision was made for technical cooperation in a number of areas: intelligence, radio communication, propaganda, and the war on merchant shipping. This clause, like that providing for mutual consultation on important operations plans, would await the test of time and mutual confidence.[16]

To decide on details of operational cooperation would probably have been premature at a time when the respective army theaters were so widely separated and the navies of the allies so differently constituted and dominated by such conflicting concepts of naval warfare.[17] The basic disagreement between the German and Japanese navies stands out sharply in a comparison of the German navy's memorandum on military cooperation with Japan of early 1941 and the Japanese-inspired military agreement of early 1942. At issue was the role which the war on enemy merchant shipping ought to play in the total war effort of the Tripartite navies. It is, of course, quite probable that the German navy would have been willing, under the circumstances of December 1941, to compromise somewhat with its earlier insistence that all efforts on land and sea be subordinated to the war on enemy merchant shipping, but the agreement of January 1942 surely fell far short of the German navy's expectations, since it obliged Japan to "strengthen her war on enemy shipping in the whole area of the Pacific and of the Indian Ocean" only in case Great Britain and the United States "concentrated [their fleets for the most part] in the Atlantic." Otherwise, Japan would presumably concentrate her naval efforts against enemy navies rather than against supply lines, in keeping with traditional Japanese naval doctrine. Germany and Italy, on the other hand, with no forces to pit against the enemy fleets, undertook to fight enemy merchant shipping in the Atlantic and Mediterranean, regardless of the concentration of enemy naval units in European or Far Eastern waters.

If there was little in the agreement that committed the powers to operational collaboration, the convention also lacked a sharply defined strategic conception. Where it ventured into the realm of strategy at all, it prescribed separate strategies for the European and Far Eastern members of the Axis. But strategy is too presumptuous a term for the vague and inconclusive prescriptions which the agreement laid down for the German and Japanese war effort. Japan, the agreement stated, would establish her supremacy in the western Pacific after seizing enemy bases and territories in Greater East Asia and destroying British and American forces in the Pacific and the Indian

Ocean. Germany's and Italy's main effort on land would aim at the enemy strongholds in the Near and Middle East.

This was far from the blueprint for the Tripartite "pincer strategy" so much feared by some Allied strategists during the early months of 1942. The German and Japanese documentation now available suggests that such a plan had not received any serious consideration by the time the military convention was signed, though the references in the pact to Japanese action in the Indian Ocean and to German-Italian offensives against the Near East were perhaps meant to prepare for an eventual juncture of the two spearheads.

What is most clearly lacking in the military agreement and the accompanying conversations is any conception of how the war might ultimately be brought to an end and how far the allies' ambitions might extend. The oversight is not surprising on the part of the Germans; since 1939, they had engaged in one campaign after another, and in spite of unanticipated military success peace still eluded them. The Japanese had shown themselves more aware of the problem of concluding a war, as the services' plan of November indicated. But the Japanese ideas of November 1941 did not find their way into the January agreement, except perhaps for the Japanese desire to see Germany shift her main war effort away from the Soviet Union and against the Western powers. However, Tokyo was to be disappointed if it had hoped to divert the German thrust from Russia merely by omitting all references to the Soviet Union from the military agreement.

During the months which followed the conclusion of the military agreement, the fortunes of war seemed to smile on the side of the Tripartite powers. Germany halted and then reversed the Russian winter offensive and the English offensive in Libya. U-boat sinkings of shipping in the Atlantic reached unprecedented totals, while the Japanese went from victory to victory in Southeast Asia. As Japanese forces gained the shores of the Indian Ocean, and German and Italian troops once more approached the borders of Egypt, both German and Japanese staffs began to give some thought to a common German-Japanese strategy that would culminate in their link-up somewhere at the shores or on the waters of the Indian Ocean.

THE VISIONS OF THE GERMAN NAVY

On the German side, the navy became the chief proponent of such an operation. Its hopes reflected both its estimates of enemy strategy and the navy's long-standing preference for an attack on the British position in the eastern Mediterranean and North Africa. Hitler's highest military advisers had initially assumed that the Pearl Harbor attack had completely changed America's strategic plans; the large-scale offensive against Europe implied in the "Victory Program," they thought, would now give way to a war strictly confined to the Pacific. Even after Roosevelt had dispelled this hope and Germany had entered the war against the United States, the German military did not expect the United States to follow a Europe-first strategy. Doubtful for some time that Britain and the United States would be able to coordinate strategy at all, the German services generally concluded by late December 1941 that Anglo-American strategy would result in a compromise between America's inclination to concentrate first on Japan and Britain's desire to move first against Italy and Germany. They expected the enemy to expend about equal strength in the defense of Singapore and of the southwest Pacific on the one hand, and in the maintenance of the British position in North Africa and the Middle East on the other. In addition, a gradual build-up of enemy forces in the Near East-India-Australia area was anticipated, from which the Western powers were expected to launch their counteroffensive against the European and Far Eastern Axis. By early 1942 it was conceded in Germany that the counteroffensive against the Axis position in Africa and Europe from this vast staging area would be launched earlier than the counterattack against Japan. Though there were slight differences in the appraisals by the different German services and by OKW, they all agreed that the enemy would disperse his efforts over a number of theaters and that a full-scale invasion of Europe in 1942 was unlikely.[18]

Allied deployment of troops and equipment during the first ten weeks of the war could only confirm the assumption that all resources would not be thrown against Germany immediately. American reinforcements to the Pacific were far heavier than American planners had anticipated before Pearl Harbor. American support for the British position in the Middle East further reduced American forces available for the primary offensive against Germany, which had been decided upon at the Arcadia Conference between Churchill and Roosevelt in December 1941–January 1942. By the end of February 1942, "the lately proclaimed strategy of concentrating all efforts first on defeating Germany had an air of unreality."[19] In early March the combined chiefs dropped the projected operation Gymnast (against

French North Africa) while during the second week of March American planners in the War Department had to scale down their estimates of American forces available in Britain after July 1942 for the cross-channel invasion then under discussion in the War Department.

Given its estimates of enemy strategy and the information available, the German navy in early 1942 thought that opportunity and necessity pointed clearly in a single direction: toward a German-Japanese attack against the still weak enemy bastions in the Near East and the Indian Ocean and the eventual resumption of direct communications between the spheres of the Tripartite powers. The navy's conclusions were set forth in a long memorandum of February 25 which was presented to Hitler in early March in shortened form.[20] Specifically, the navy recommended that Germany capture the Suez Canal in 1942, by an advance either through Egypt or across the Caucasus or preferably both. Japan was expected to wrest control of the Indian Ocean from the enemy, who was to be given the *coup de grâce* by Axis-inspired and Axis-led independence movements in the Arab world and India.

The arguments marshaled by the navy in favor of this enterprise were profuse and contradictory. It was held that such an operation might end the war against England; on the other hand, the navy argued that the Suez operation and the link-up with the Japanese was particularly necessary if the Tripartite powers wanted to consolidate their positions for a long drawn-out conflict. Only if communications were opened and the oil of the Near East exchanged for the raw materials of East Asia, it was argued, could the war economies of Germany and Japan be made impregnable. Both offensive and defensive merits were ascribed to the plan: the enemy was still weak in the area and could be more easily overcome in 1942 than in a later year; at the same time, the enemy's build-up in the area, if permitted to proceed unchallenged, would eventually threaten the flanks of Germany, Italy, and Japan.

The navy's memorandum implied that Germany was to take the first step in this grandiose scheme. Only when Germany's offensive preparations against the Near East had become clear was Japan expected to start her battle for the control of the Indian Ocean.[21] Before approaching the Japanese, therefore, the German navy had to secure the Führer's and the other services' agreement to its plan. At first, the navy's prospects looked bright. When Admiral Erich Raeder, the navy's commander-in-chief, had first presented the gist of the navy memorandum to Hitler during a conference in mid-February 1942, he had obtained the Führer's qualified approval. In early March, a few days after receiving the navy's memorandum, Hitler indicated to the naval staff that he approved of their ideas "in principle."[22] But he did hardly more than that. In the absence of a specific directive by Hitler, the navy was unable to proceed with staff studies which required consultation with German authorities outside the navy, or with the Italian staffs whose cooperation would be necessary.[23] While Hitler pursued plans for an early summer offensive in North Africa in conversations with Mussolini in April, he did not think Germany and Italy capable of the capture of Suez. Speaking to Mussolini in late April, he considered Suez as no more than a "desirable future goal" (*ein erstrebenswertes Zukunftsziel*).[24] In early May, OKW decided that the North African offensive should not cross the Egyptian frontier, even if Tobruk had been conquered. Hitler was not visibly enthusiastic about the projected capture of Malta, yet without it Axis supply lines to Africa would remain too precarious to permit a large-scale offensive into Egypt. In all, it looked during the spring as if no determined Axis push for the Suez Canal would be made in 1942.[25]

While the navy failed to get energetic support for its plan from the Führer, the other services and OKW also withheld their approval. OKW's specific objections to the navy memorandum are unknown, but the navy had found as early as February that OKW was cool to the idea of strategic cooperation with Japan. A month later, an internal navy memorandum of March 21 again found that "OKW . . . seems to place no value on joint strategic or operational planning with the Japanese."[26] The navy probably failed to appreciate OKW's absorption in Hitler's plans for a new summer offensive in Russia, though OKM (Supreme Command of the German Navy) itself had by no means suggested that the Russian theater be neglected. In fact, the navy considered the acquisition of the oil of the Caucasus as a necessary prerequisite for the Near Eastern operation it advocated; it viewed the capture of the Caucasus range itself at least as a desirable precondition for a double-pronged attack against the Middle East. Without bringing OKW round to the navy's favored Suez operation, the memorandum of the naval staff may have reinforced Hitler's and the OKW's desire to commit Germany's main force in 1942 to the southern sector of the Russian front, at the expense of the central front where the OKH (Supreme Command of the German Army) wished to see German forces concentrated. The OKW directive of early April which outlined the operations plan for the 1942 campaign in Russia justified the southern emphasis with a reference to the access to the Near East which might be gained via the Caucasus.[27]

Nor did the navy's memorandum find favor with the army high command. In a short comment delivered to the navy in early April, General Halder explained that operations beyond the Caucasus in 1942 were out of the question and that an offensive against Egypt, though perhaps temporarily successful, would also prove too hazardous unless the British position in the Near East could be attacked from both the west and the northeast simultaneously. To OKH, the impossibility of one operation canceled out the other, even though the navy for the time being refused to accept this argument.[28]

As long as the German navy's plan made little headway with the other services, OKW, or Hitler himself, the navy could not embark on joint planning with the Japanese. In its conferences with Japanese naval representatives in Berlin, the German naval staff in fact could speak only in the most general terms of its interest in joint German-Japanese action in the area of the Near East and India.

The Japanese may have sensed the lack of German enthusiasm. In December the Germans had failed to push military cooperation to more intimate levels, beyond the draft agreement presented by Japan, no doubt disappointing those Japanese military who favored closely coordinated moves into the Indian Ocean. The German difficulties at the Russian front at the same time raised the question whether Germany had the resources—not to mention the will—to engage a substantial number of her troops in a drive against the British position in the Middle East. Finally, during January and February, German military planning may well have appeared at a standstill, since the navy hardly went beyond vague references to an eventual breakthrough into the Near East.

The German navy's frustration with the slowness and obstinacy of its sister services and its superiors in the Führer's headquarters must have increased during February, when Japanese naval representatives in Berlin and Tokyo began to show a keener interest than before in the Indian Ocean. By February 10, the Japanese navy had asked the German naval staff for maps or data on Ceylon which the German services might be willing to share with the Japanese. Within ten days the German navy turned over relevant material to the Japanese; if the Japanese could be made to land in Ceylon, the German navy may have argued, this would strengthen the navy's hand in persuading Hitler to accept the navy's pet scheme, just then under study at the Führer's headquarters. Admiral Naokuni Nomura, who represented Japan on the Tripartite military committee in Berlin, simultaneously warned the German navy that Japan would consider her westward operations pointless unless Germany carried the war into the Near East with full force, a warning which could not but heighten the German navy's sense of urgency about the matters which it was just then setting down in its long memorandum for Hitler.[29]

Further indications of a Japanese interest in the Indian Ocean and of impending Japanese military action in that theater reached the German navy during the second half of February, when the Japanese submitted a request for submarine bases in Madagascar.[30] Simultaneously, Japanese newspapers began to call for an invasion of the Indian Ocean, and Premier Tojo invited the Indian people to join the Japanese co-prosperity sphere.[31] The Japanese capture of Singapore on February 15 and the rapid progress of her offensive in Burma, leading to the capture of Rangoon on March 8, confirmed the German navy in its belief that Japan was about to move farther westward, quite possibly to Ceylon.

Leading German naval circles thought at the time, and some German naval historians have argued since, that during February 1942 the Japanese were ready and eager to cooperate strategically and tactically with Germany to conquer the British position in the Near East and India. According to their view, the blame for missing this opportunity rested with the Germans, particularly Hitler and OKW, who proved indifferent, so the story goes, to the plans espoused by the German navy and the Japanese military. The view has been expressed most succinctly by a member of the former German naval staff. Writing after the war, Admiral Kurt Assmann maintained that in February 1942 Japan stood "ready to attack the British position based on Suez [*die britische Machtposition in Grossraum von Suez*] from the East, if the Axis powers would launch a corresponding offensive from the west."[32]

DOUBTS AND DIVISIONS IN THE JAPANESE CAMP

In fact, however, the Japanese attitude was not so certain. Deliberations on grand strategy during the early months of 1942 suggested that the Japanese were much more sharply divided than the German navy thought. In Japan, as in Germany, advocates of a joint German-Japanese offensive had to battle formidable advocates of other strategies, to whom they eventually succumbed.

As early as January 1942 most of Japan's military leaders seem to have assumed that the first phase of their war plan was certain of success and that it was merely a matter of time before Japan established herself along the so-called "defense perimeter" set as the initial goal of operations.[33] In other words, they were taking for granted the conquest of the Philippines, the Dutch East Indies, Malaya, and Burma, and even assuming that it would be completed before the end of March, several weeks ahead of schedule. The rapid and easy successes of the first weeks made planning for the second stage of the war all the more urgent.

Formally, it was the task of Imperial General Headquarters to formulate the strategy for this, as for the earlier phase of the war. Actually, all the initial planning occurred within the services separately. Once the general and naval staffs had approved the separate studies and proposals of their respective services, the army and navy sections in Imperial General Headquarters would be called upon to adjust these plans to one another.

Adjustment proved difficult, as the two services attempted, during the month of February in particular, to agree on the basic assumptions that ought to underlie all future operations. Navy spokesmen advocated bold advances beyond the defense perimeter as originally defined. The army would go no further than small-scale local moves beyond the original line. While neither service advocated hostilities with Russia, the army claimed to have to keep substantial numbers of troops in reserve since hostilities with the

Soviet Union could never be ruled out. An unsatisfactory compromise on the scope of future operations—more verbal than real—was worked out in Imperial General Headquarters in early March and confirmed by a liaison conference.[34]

Meanwhile the separate services had been working on more specific operational plans that would have to be accommodated within whatever general formula Headquarters should prove able to devise. Since most of the operations possible for Japan involved primarily the navy, naval planners took the initiative in proposals for the second-stage operations. The most active and inventive planners within the navy were to be found on the staff of the Combined Fleet, though the final responsibility for war plans rested with the chief of naval operations, Admiral Osami Nagano. The Combined Fleet, by virtue of its power, must have a voice in whatever decisions were made, whether to challenge directly the remaining units of the American navy or to concentrate on further amphibious landings. In addition, the Combined Fleet planners commanded a respect born of the early successes of the war, in particular the operation against Pearl Harbor, which had been the brainchild of the Combined Fleet's commander, Admiral Isoroku Yamamoto (and had been only reluctantly approved by Admiral Nagano). Strike power and a record of success assured the Combined Fleet the dominant role in the navy's strategic planning for the second phase of operations.[35]

Admiral Natome Ugaki, chief of staff to Admiral Yamamoto, took the initiative. Pondering the problems of Japan's future action on his flagship in Hiroshima Bay in mid-January, Ugaki decided for an offensive rather than a defensive conduct of the war.

Considering offensive action in the direction of Australia, India, or Hawaii, Ugaki at first decided on Hawaii. His chief reason seems to have been the realization that time was working against Japan and that, to win the war, she would have to hit the United States where it hurt most and as early as possible, while America was still weak from her losses at Pearl Harbor and the lateness of her drive to arm. He sought above all to destroy the American fleet and to capture its most important and most advanced Pacific base, Pearl Harbor. Germany's future plans of action were secondary in his thinking. If anything, Ugaki's assessment of the German future strengthened his "eastern" orientation. In his diary, he recorded as the fourth of four reasons which impelled him to his chosen course the consideration that, in the event Germany defeated Britain, strong British naval forces might join the American fleet in the Pacific. This possibility, according to Ugaki, made it all the more necessary that Japan move quickly and decisively against the American navy.[36]

Having arrived at this conclusion in a few days of quiet deliberation, Ugaki submitted his proposals to his planners and asked for more detailed studies as well as a final estimate of his own views. The planners of Ugaki's staff in the end disagreed with their chief and judged that because of the lack of any surprise element and because of insufficient Japanese air strength over Hawaii in the face of American ship- and shore-based batteries, such a landing was too risky.[37]

Concurring with the considered opinion of his staff, Ugaki next commissioned his planners to investigate the possibilities for a large Japanese offensive in the Indian Ocean. The switch in Ugaki's ideas is hard to time,[38] but it probably coincided with the marked increase of Japan's interest in the Indian Ocean which the German naval staff began to observe in early February. It should be remembered, however, that what the German navy (and Admiral Assmann in his retrospective evaluation) took to be evidence of fully matured Japanese intentions was no more than plans under study by only *one* admittedly influential branch of *one* of Japan's services.

Actually, the Combined Fleet's planning for a westward offensive went through two stages. First, the plan assumed that Japanese moves would be closely coordinated with German operations. When this assumption had to be dropped (at a time which is still hard to pinpoint), the Combined Fleet elaborated plans looking toward a unilateral move into the Indian Ocean. The details are best told in the words of two Japanese naval historians, Mitsuo Fuchida and Masatake Okumiya:

> In view of these unfavorable findings [concerning the Hawaii operation], Admiral Ugaki reluctantly set aside his plan and directed the Combined Fleet staff to begin studying an alternative scheme of offensive operations to the West, advanced by Senior Fleet Operations Officer Captain Kameto Kuroshima. Ugaki, who did not fully concur in Kuroshima's idea, instructed that the study be carried out subject to the following conditions:
>
> 1. Although there appeared to be no imminent danger of Soviet hostilities, sufficient precautions should be taken to meet such an eventuality.
> 2. Similarly, adequate measures should be provided to suppress hit-and-run attacks by United States carrier task forces from the east.
> 3. Launching of any operations to the west should await refitting of the naval forces following com-

> pletion of the first-phase operations and also should be timed to synchronize with German offensives in the Near and Middle East.
>
> 4. The objectives of the western operations would have to be clearly defined from the start. They would be (*a*) destruction of the British fleet, (*b*) capture of strategic points and elimination of enemy bases, and (*c*) establishment of contact between Japanese and European Axis forces.
>
> Thus, the Combined Fleet began its study of the Kuroshima plan with the idea that the proposed westward operations would be part of a closely coordinated Axis offensive from two directions. However, this concept suffered an early setback when the headquarters received a copy of the new tripartite Axis military agreement concluded on January 19. The agreement, though it made passing reference to Germany's advance eastward and Japan's advance westward, said nothing at all with regard to a future joint offensive effort. Ugaki was keenly disappointed and concluded that, rather than attempt to coordinate her action with that of the European Axis, Japan could best promote overall Axis success by fixing her own strategy independently.
>
> Hence, the idea of a joint offensive was abandoned, and Combined Fleet continued its study of the western operations as a purely Japanese project.[39]

This passage presents several difficulties. For one, it is difficult to see why receipt of a copy of the military alliance of January 19 should have produced the effect on the Combined Fleet which is here attributed to it. The alliance had, after all, been a Japanese idea from the beginning and the Germans had done nothing to add to or detract from its strategic provisions.

Two solutions to this at first rather puzzling account by the two Japanese historians may be suggested. If the Japanese treaty draft had originated in the Japanese naval or army general staffs without the knowledge of the Combined Fleet's staff, the Combined Fleet may not have realized that the treaty belatedly submitted to them was really a product of Japanese, not German, initiative. In this case, it would be understandable that the Combined Fleet would attach an exaggerated significance to the treaty text as an indication of German aims.[40]

A second explanation assumes that the Combined Fleet knew of the real origin of the treaty draft and that the draft had, in fact, been intended to test German willingness to cooperate closely with Japan. When the Combined Fleet saw the treaty text and realized that Germany was unwilling to go beyond the very loose coordination proposed in that document, it modified the Kuroshima plan, which was predicated on much closer cooperation with Berlin.

The account by the Japanese historians presents further difficulties when we look at the matter of timing. The Japanese knew as early as the first part of January that Germany would accept the Japanese draft in substantially its original form, even though the formal signing was delayed until January 18. Why should it have taken the Combined Fleet until February to discover the text of the pact and hence learn of the unlikelihood of very close cooperation with Germany? A correlation of the approximate dates found in the Japanese account with the more precise dates in the German naval records suggests that it was not the disclosure of the alliance text, but other developments in Berlin, which caused the Combined Fleet to modify the Kuroshima plan.

First and foremost, Germany failed to respond to the warning which Admiral Nomura had delivered in Berlin on February 10, according to which Japan's own plans for a western offensive would be abandoned or curtailed unless Germany joined in an attack on the British position in the Middle East and India. The Germans, to be sure, made data on Ceylon available and promised to intervene at Vichy in the matter of Madagascan bases,[41] hoping as they did to see Japan move westward. But these were clearly minor measures of support for a unilateral Japanese move. No assurances of a major reorientation of strategy from the Russian front to the Middle East were forthcoming in February, and in mid-February discussions of the "pincer strategy" between Admiral Nomura and OKW were postponed until later in the spring.[42]

Whether the Kuroshima plan in its initial form was abandoned before the end of February or early in March is not clear. The German records suggest a final attempt by the naval staff and the Combined Fleet in early March to get a German commitment for action in the Middle East during the forthcoming summer. A delegation of Combined Fleet officers called on the German naval attaché on March 2 and presented the following considerations:

> At the present stage of the war the decision about the strategy to be used by the tripartite powers could be of decisive importance. Should we succeed in the next few months in establishing a link between East Asia and Europe via the Indian Ocean, the war would be practically won and the British Empire would be finished. But this breakthrough would have to occur soon in order to bring the war to a speedy and happy conclusion. At a later time the link-up would be very much harder to achieve in view of the rearmament of the Anglo-Americans.

> The question therefore arose whether Germany should not also concentrate her forces on this aim. . . . If a simultaneous defeat of Russia and the opening of the route to the Indian Ocean were not possible, it was perhaps advisable to postpone the final destruction of the Soviet Union and to try to come to an arrangement with her on a basis acceptable to Germany. . . . The Japanese fleet would be occupied until the end of April with mopping-up operations in the southern area and with the necessary replacements and repairs. But then the fleet was available for a joint operation from the west and the east against Suez and the Near East on the one hand, the Indian Ocean on the other. If the German government agreed to this program, Japan was ready at any time to mediate between her and the Soviet Union.[43]

Berlin's answer made clear that Japan could not count on a commitment of significant German strength to the Near Eastern theater. Delivered within the week, Germany's reply maintained that a truce with Russia was out of the question, but that a Japanese move into the Indian Ocean would be welcome.[44] With no German commitment about the extent or timing of Germany's contribution to such a venture, Japan must have considered the answer a polite refusal.

The failure of its attempt caused the Combined Fleet merely to change its plans for an Indian Ocean offensive, not to abandon them. The naval staff was won to the Combined Fleet's idea of a unilateral Japanese operation in the Indian Ocean, table-top maneuvers were held, and in mid-March the navy approached the army section of Imperial General Headquarters with an official request to consider the proposed operation. The navy's plan aimed at the destruction of the British fleet, the capture of Ceylon, and the acquisition of air control in the Indian Ocean. These operations were placed in a broader strategic framework, designed "to safeguard the Dutch East Indies and Malaya against a threat from the West and to facilitate an early juncture with German forces in the Near East."[45]

The Japanese Army, not Germany, killed this plan. As Fuchida and Okumiya laconically state: "The army's refusal to cooperate meant that the proposed offensive in the Indian Ocean could not be carried out."[46] Since the army would have a larger part to play in the Indian Ocean offensive than in attacks on smaller island groups or naval action in the Pacific, its refusal doomed the plan. The army's decision probably reflected its general reluctance to carry the war far beyond the original defense perimeter. In addition, the army also believed that military action on Soviet soil was not entirely impossible in 1942, particularly if Germany once more concentrated all her forces in a vast summer campaign against Russia. Furthermore, the army's experience in China may have caused it to fear that military operations in Ceylon or India would lead to political anarchy in the Indian subcontinent and possibly its bolshevization.[47]

Whether the army's veto was significantly affected by what it knew of German plans for 1942 cannot be reconstructed. The army never had a chance to pass on the Kuroshima plan in its first stage, where simultaneous German operations were assumed. The army's veto seems more likely to have been grounded in the general caution of that service than in consideration of the German plans.

The further evidence that Germany would not relegate the Soviet theater to second place, which became available to Japan in mid-March, may, however, have strengthened some naval opponents of the westward offensive. On March 14, the German naval staff informed the Japanese naval representative in Berlin for the first time of the existence and general contents of the navy's memorandum of February 25. At the same time, the German navy made clear that the memorandum had not yet received Hitler's approval and that interservice discussions had not yet begun. The extent and timing of German operations in the Near East, the German navy explained, would depend on the outcome of the Russian campaign, which had first priority.[48]

The effect of these disclosures on the Japanese navy is not clear, but it was a fact that in the navy, too, important groups doubted that the westward operation was the most useful employment of Japanese resources. Within the naval general staff itself, planning had looked toward a Japanese advance in a southeasterly direction with the aim of cutting American-Australian supply lines, before the Combined Fleet's proposal for westward operations had been adopted. The Combined Fleet's own commander, Admiral Yamamoto, was obsessed by the fear of American hit-and-run attacks against Japan's eastern defenses, and perhaps against the home islands themselves.[49] He, for one, quickly turned to the elaboration of new plans for an eastward offensive once the army had turned down the western plan.

For a moment in late March it looked as if the Japanese navy had after all decided to launch its campaign in the Indian Ocean. When part of the Combined Fleet moved west, the British could fear and the Germans hope that a landing on Ceylon was in the making. The Japanese bombed the naval base at

Trincomalee and a number of open cities, but they were not about to land. The operation, decided upon in early March, bore no relation to the discussion of grand strategy; the aim was the limited one of protecting the Japanese sea lanes to Burma.[50] Certainly, as long as the British fleet in the Indian Ocean was still in existence, a landing would carry the same risks as did the Hawaiian operation rejected earlier. The Japanese would have liked to engage the British fleet, but the British, too weak to give battle, withdrew into the depths of the Indian Ocean with few losses and eluded the Japanese.

After the middle of April, the chances of a Japanese landing in Ceylon, which was, in turn, the prerequisite for Japanese naval action in the western Indian Ocean, grew dimmer, although the British could not be sure of this immediately. Events hastened a decision on strategy. The Doolittle raid of April 18 on Tokyo confirmed the worst fears of Admiral Yamamoto about the dangers still threatening the home islands from carrier-based enemy aircraft. It forced the Japanese services to reconcile their differences about the objectives of an eastern offensive and led to the choice of the Midway operation, advocated by the Combined Fleet after its abandonment of the western operation; the naval staff's preferred offensive against the supply line to Australia took second place.[51] The Indian Ocean receded further into the background in Japanese strategic thinking when British forces landed in Madagascar in early May, forestalling a possible future Japanese foothold on the island.

Once Japanese landing attempts beyond the original perimeter had led to serious losses, particularly in carriers and the naval air arm, during the battles of the Coral Sea and of Midway (May 8 and June 3–6 respectively), the Indian Ocean became a purely defensive front for the Japanese. Germany had already been informed in April that for Japan the Pacific took precedence over the Indian Ocean; by early May, Berlin was likewise told that the capture of Ceylon had been postponed.[52]

THE AFTERLIFE OF A VISION

The most favorable moment for Axis offensives toward the western Indian Ocean had now passed. German and Japanese representatives continued to emphasize the desirability of such a joint operation but, lacking the prerequisites of action and serious planning, their discussions turned into tedious and unproductive repetitions of the same theme. Arguments on either side varied but slightly during the rest of the spring and summer. As neither side was ready to fulfill the tasks its spokesmen had once so grandly assumed, both began to insist that the first step toward the joint operation was up to the other side. The Japanese promised action against Ceylon if and when German troops appeared at Suez or south of the Caucasus; the German navy now insisted, contrary to its argument in the February memorandum, that Germany would move into the Near East only after, not before, the Japanese had attacked enemy sea lanes in the western Indian Ocean.[53]

To the Allies, the danger of an Axis "pincer movement" into the Near East threatened once more in late June, when the Germans captured Tobruk and seemed ready to drive on to the Suez Canal. In Japan, too, the German victory revived the idea of an amphibious landing in Ceylon.[54] But Rommel's capture of Tobruk had not been anticipated in Berlin, and no preparations had been made to extend it into a conquest of Egypt. Moreover, the German offensive beyond Tobruk had come to a halt by early July. It could not be resumed without a drastic improvement in the German-Italian supply route across the Mediterranean. With the battle in Africa reduced to a contest of two supply systems, the German navy urged the Japanese throughout that summer to cut enemy supply lines in the western Indian Ocean. Such action, the navy insisted, would reduce the resistance both of Russia and of Britain in Africa, and was a necessary precondition to a German push into the Middle East.[55]

Serious military reverses further exposed the emptiness of the German-Japanese joint warfare. Through much of the summer and fall, the Germans and the Japanese plied each other with preposterous suggestions about their own and each other's future conduct of the war. Unaware of the serious Japanese losses at the Coral Sea and at Midway, the German naval high command argued as late as July that Japan might with impunity neglect her Pacific defenses since the Pacific was completely safe. Japan should use not only submarines, but "the whole weight of [her] fleet," in the Indian Ocean, the Germans thought.[56] Even after the American landings on Guadalcanal in early August, the Germans still demanded that Japan subordinate her Pacific defenses to the "focal point of over-all warfare," to wit, the Indian Ocean.[57]

Similarly, the German military gave Japan a quite unrealistic picture of what Nippon might expect from her ally. A German offensive across the Caucasus was pictured as imminent in August, though by September and October the Germans were explaining that its date had been postponed to early 1943. Nor were these prospects dangled before the Japanese merely to strengthen Nippon's morale; German leaders, including Hitler, thought these operations possible.[58] Little wonder that the Japanese retained their misconceptions about the state of Germany's eastern front. In early September, Admiral Nomura suggested that during the "winter lull" in the fighting on the eastern front, the capture of Suez might yet be accomplished. Though the British victory at El Alamein and the Allied landings in North Africa in early November worried the Japanese, the remedies they proposed were quite unrealistic. Early in the fourth week of November, Nomura was alternately suggesting a German attack on Gibraltar and a German push into Iran and via Iraq to the Suez Canal in order to eliminate the Allied menace from North Africa.[59] These were the very days when Russian troops were completing their encirclement of the sixth army in Stalingrad, and when Japanese surface ships were being withdrawn from the Indian Ocean to be available for the battle of the Solomons.

The autumn of 1942 was a time of mutual recrimination as well as of unreal proposals. While the Germans and Japanese argued over who was responsible for letting British supplies reach Egypt, the Italians blamed the defeat of El Alamein on the inactivity of Japanese submarines in the Indian Ocean.[60]

Only gradually did a more realistic appraisal of the common situation and of the remaining opportunities for cooperation gain the upper hand. In early December, the German naval high command belatedly and ponderously observed that

> the demands made on the tripartite forces in their ex-

> tended spheres of living have risen so much that in the foreseeable future [*auf absehbare Zeit*] offensive operations aimed at the cooperation of the allied land and air forces or the communication between Europe and East Asia do not seem possible.[61]

Yet not all German military authorities were prepared for such a verdict. OKW, at any rate, phrased its estimate in a more hopeful tone and expressed confidence that an offensive against the Middle East would be resumed at the earliest possible date.[62] When the German naval attaché in Tokyo reported in December that Japan's fortunes hung on the defense of the Solomons and that an expedition into the Indian Ocean was quite out of the question after "the heavy setbacks of Midway and the Solomons," he was severely reprimanded by OKW for his "psychologically dangerous" pessimism.[63]

In the end, plans for German-Japanese cooperation assumed a more modest shape in 1943 than they had had during the preceding spring. The Germans tried to get the Japanese more heavily committed to the war on enemy merchant shipping in the Indian Ocean. They no longer pictured such attacks as a necessary first step toward a joint offensive against India, but as one of the few remaining means by which the Axis might decide the war in its favor.[64] Whatever the outcome of these more modest efforts, strategic initiative had passed out of the hands of the Tripartite powers by late 1942. To the German naval staff and certain officers in the Japanese navy it could appear only as a loss by default.

THE PARTITION OF THE WORLD

3

Throughout their four and one-half years of alliance, German and Japanese statesmen assured each other and the world that their respective ambitions for empire conflicted nowhere. Mutual recognition of each other's New Orders was written into the first two articles of the Tripartite Pact, and similar assurances were exchanged during the subsequent war years. Among the Axis's opponents, the assurances aroused only skepticism, for the appetite of each of the partners was judged too ravenous to be curbed by self-restraint. For the diplomatic historian, an answer to the question requires an understanding of just what role territorial issues and agreements did play in the alliance. Were the territorial objectives of each alliance partner clearly defined and understood by the other? Did territorial ambitions fluctuate with the shifting military fortunes of the allies? How smoothly was formal agreement on territorial matters reached and to what extent did disagreements retard cooperation on the diplomatic or military level? This chapter explores Axis plans for a new division of the world, and the relation of such plans to the other dimensions of the alliance.

ASSIGNMENT OF THE SPOILS

During the weeks of internal deliberation and mutual probing which preceded the conclusion of the Tripartite Pact, the Japanese sought a recognition of their future New Order more anxiously than the Germans did of theirs. The Japanese were almost certain that Germany would raise no question about China's and Manchukuo's political place in the Japanese sphere, but they anticipated renewed German attempts to obtain a special status for German business there. What alarmed the Japanese most during the summer of 1940 was the idea that Germany might have political designs of her own on one or another of the European colonies in Southeast Asia whose mother countries she had either already conquered (Holland, France) or seemed about to invade (Great Britain). Neither a German declaration of disinterestedness in the Dutch East Indies on May 22, 1940,[1] nor the provisions of the Franco-German armistice of June 22, 1940, which left the French government in nominal control of its overseas colonies but gave Germany a voice in determining the colonies' military defenses, had done much to allay Japanese suspicions. In the conferences of the summer of 1940, in which Japan defined her program for negotiations with Berlin, the question of her future hegemony in East and Southeast Asia therefore played a prominent role.

The Japanese statesmen were anxious to obtain German recognition for the greatest possible Japanese control of Southeast Asia. Concerning the extent of territory to be controlled, the Japanese services insisted that Burma and the eastern part of India, as well as Australia and New Zealand in the east, be included in Greater East Asia. Nevertheless, it was agreed that Germany need not be told immediately of these ambitious boundaries, and that a more limited definition of Greater East Asia, exclusive of India and Australia and New Zealand, would be used in the forthcoming negotiations. Concerning the kind of control, military and civilian representatives were also agreed that Germany must promise to recognize both Japan's political and economic hegemony in her "sphere."

Once negotiations had begun in Tokyo on September 9, Matsuoka found it tactically prudent to present Japan's territorial demands in general rather than in specific terms; the German negotiators proved neither niggardly nor inquisitive and immediately conceded the Japanese requests without inquiring into their limits or implications.[2] Then the negotiators turned quickly to the precise terms of the military alliance, which, judging from the time they gave it, interested them much more. Amid the unreal disposal of whole countries, a single episode threatened to bring the conversations down to earth. Matsuoka wanted explicit German recognition of Japan's possession of the former German colonies in the Pacific north of the equator and a promise of the islands south of the equator presently mandated to Britain, Australia, and New Zealand. The matter was finally settled in one of the secret exchanges appended to the pact without the knowledge of the German government. Instead of ceding to Japan the islands mandated to her, Germany promised to transfer them to Japan after the war for a compensation; the possessions now mandated to the British would revert to Germany after the war, whereupon Berlin would be prepared to dispose of them in Japan's favor, again for a compensation. The negotiations about the former German islands in the Pacific illustrate one of the paradoxes of Axis territorial provisions: while thousands of square miles were disposed of in the September talks without exact delimitation, the negotiations on the mandated islands became so detailed that the negotiators even suggested the token price Japan might pay for outright sovereignty over the northern islands: six sacks of coffee.[3] If nothing else, the principle of compensation for former German holdings had been salvaged.

In the Tripartite Pact, Germany and Japan divided large parts of the world between them without a mutual understanding of the precise terms of the bargain. The geographic limits of the spheres were left undefined, and the term "leadership," by which the control of the signatories over the areas in their respective New Orders was expressed, remained elusive. No doubt Matsuoka had good reason not to insist on clarification: once Japan's troops were ready to move into the areas vaguely but firmly conceded to her by Germany, Japan would be able to define the boundaries and the measure of her control at will. But what induced the Germans to treat these territorial matters in such a cavalier manner? Of course, Hitler had been known earlier to "cede" to prospective friends large territories not yet under his control. In September 1940, however, Berlin's preoccupation with securing a military alliance against America probably explained the German concessions on all territorial issues. But if this is true, the Germans played their cards clumsily. They promised to acknowledge Japan's Greater East Asia before negotiations about a military alliance had begun in earnest and then had nothing to trade for the alliance but a waiver clause which practically invalidated it.

Since the Nazi record is not marked by generosity, we may wonder whether the Germans acted in good faith when they assigned all Southeast Asia to the Japanese sphere. The German record is somewhat contradictory, but the main outlines of Germany's immediate territorial ambitions in the summer of 1940 are clear enough. In June and early July, when Hitler still hoped for a peace with the English in the near future, his territorial demands overseas would probably have been limited. His main demand, clearly, would have been for a free hand in eastern Europe.[4] By the second half of July, when the prospect of a war to the finish with the British Empire had been accepted, plans for a large German colonial empire in Central Africa, at the expense of the French, the Belgians, and the British, flourished among the German leaders. The farthest eastward extension of German power, according to German naval plans of July and September 1940, would have included the English and French island groups in the Indian Ocean—Madagascar and the Comoro Islands were to be taken from France, the Seychelles group and Mauritius from Britain. There is no evidence that Germany at that time contemplated taking over either French or British colonies in Asia.[5] In fact, Hitler seems to have realized that several other nations were more strategically situated to take advantage of the disintegration of British power in Asia. In July he had already given it as his opinion that only Japan and the United States would benefit if the British Empire disintegrated as a result of a German conquest of the British Isles.[6] In regard to Britain's holdings in the Far East, therefore, the treaty text consigning the Far East to the Japanese sphere of control seems to have accorded closely with Hitler's own earlier estimate of the limitations of German power in Asia.

But possible German designs on British colonies in Asia had been only one source of Japanese concern. While beleaguered Britain held out during the summer and fall of 1940, the disposition of her colonial holdings was in any case an academic question. Japan was more concerned about the Asian colonial holdings of France and Holland, powers already defeated by Germany. With Vichy subject to German pressure, Berlin might either hinder or help Japan's advance into French Indo-China. From June to August 1940, when Japan negotiated with French and French Indo-Chinese authorities about the right to establish *de facto* control over the northern part of the colony, Berlin had maintained a nice neutrality between Vichy and Tokyo, both of which besieged the Germans with requests for diplomatic support.[7]

If the German attitude toward Indo-China had kept Japanese suspicions alive during July and August, the promises conveyed to the Japanese government by Minister Stahmer in early September must have quieted Japan's fears, particularly as the German recognition of Japan's political hegemony in the Far East was soon backed by deeds. In the face of strong French pleas, Berlin refused to sanction the military reinforcement of Indo-China and in this manner eased the Japanese entry into the northern part of the colony during the fourth week of September. She did not, however, bring direct pressure to bear on Vichy on Japan's behalf during the autumn. In subsequent months, Berlin continued to aid Japan's penetration of French Indo-China. In January and February 1941, when Japan sought to mediate the Indo-Chinese-Thai dispute, and in July 1941, when she sought to extend her protectorate over the southern part of the colony, the German government gave some support to Tokyo.[8] Obviously Germany's desire to see Japan attack Singapore and engage Great Britain in war explains why Berlin lent its diplomatic support to the Japanese penetration of Southeast Asia.

GERMAN BACK DOORS TO SOUTHEAST ASIA

While Japanese fears of German *political* designs on French Indo-China did not materialize, Japan was proved wrong in her estimate that the Reich would more easily let go of its *economic* than of its political interests in the French colony. Shortly after the conclusion of the Tripartite Pact, prolonged and disagreeable disputes arose between the two allies over their respective economic stakes in Indo-China. The source of these disputes was not so much bad faith on either side as the extreme haste and superficiality with which the German negotiators of the Tripartite Pact had committed their government to whatever interpretation the Japanese chose to put on the very flexible term of their "leadership" in Greater East Asia. The failure of the German negotiators to keep their government sufficiently informed of the course of negotiations and of the annexes to the pact probably also contributed to the tensions that soon arose over rival economic claims in French Indo-China.

Minister Stahmer's assertions in Tokyo, for instance, had led the Japanese to believe that Germany was ready to conduct her economic relations with countries in Greater East Asia in the future only in consultation with, and perhaps even through the agency of, the Japanese. Probably they had read more than was warranted into Stahmer's declaration to Matsuoka on September 9, 1940:

> Of course Germany recognizes and respects Japan's political leadership in Greater East Asia. All she wants in these regions is of an economic nature, and she is ready to cooperate with Japan to further her aims. Naturally she looks to Japan to do her best to accommodate German enterprises and to enable Germany to obtain in these regions materials she needs and may need.[9]

Shortly after the conclusion of the Tripartite Pact, however, it became apparent to the Japanese that the German government had no intention of abandoning bilateral negotiations with countries in Greater East Asia. This was true of both Thailand and French Indo-China, but Indo-China became the thornier issue because the German government, through its control over Vichy, was able to obtain economic rights there which the Japanese were determined to resist. The bone of contention between the allies was a Franco-German economic agreement, probably of September 1940, by which the French guaranteed to Germany roughly two-fifths of the Indo-Chinese rubber production for the coming year, in addition to a sizable share of France's own rubber quota, which was fixed at approximately a quarter of the total harvest. Under the Franco-German agreement, the Reich was expected to satisfy Italian and Japanese demands out of the German quota.[10]

The Japanese resented the agreement, not only as a threat to the amount of rubber they could import from the French colony, but also as an improper interference with their own hegemony in Asia. By late October 1940, Japan formally demanded a German guarantee that no agreements concerning Indo-China or the Dutch East Indies would be concluded by Berlin without prior consultation, a demand maintained through 1941.[11] The Japanese demand gave the German government an opportunity to explain what role it expected to play in Japan's future New Order. In early December 1940, Ambassador Ott was instructed to inform the Japanese that

> Germany . . . expects that when the new order is established in the Greater East Asia sphere her economic interests will be preserved as well as the right independently to make arrangements regarding these interests with areas where political authority is not

> exercised by Japanese organs, and to effect business transactions in these areas.[12]

A few weeks later, Ott was instructed to avoid henceforth the term Greater East Asia "sphere" (in favor of "area"), since its use might imply tacit recognition of a greater degree of Japanese control than Germany was willing to admit.[13]

The Japanese would not change their stand on the principle at issue. Nor was Germany willing to give way on the question of principle, even while practical considerations of distance and transportation and Japan's partial control over the raw-material production of the French colony compelled her to modify her actual negotiating procedures. Greater respect was paid to Japanese sensitivities in 1941, but the issue itself was not resolved. The German Foreign Ministry in Berlin, in contrast with some of its agents in the Far East, insisted that Germany's right to negotiate directly with countries under Japanese leadership not be compromised, even though concessions in procedure were permissible. Some officials in the German Foreign Ministry indignantly rejected the Japanese position as one more example of Nipponese impudence; others emphasized, more soberly, that this was not the time to risk a quarrel with Tokyo. A memorandum of late March 1941 nicely illustrates the German position:

> Since the conclusion of the Tripartite Pact, the Japanese have claimed the role of leader and middleman not only in Manchuria and China, but beyond that in respect to German economic relations with Indo-China, Thailand, and the Netherlands East Indies. We have officially protested against this claim in a declara-

> tion by State Secretary Weizsäcker to Ambassador Kurusu. The question of the nature of Japan's leadership has not been pursued, since for the time being we have no interest in such a discussion, and since during the war we practically depend largely on the goodwill of the Japanese government for transport of goods from the said countries, camouflage via Japanese firms, and transport by Japanese ships.[14]

The German government eventually followed this line of reasoning and even, through pressure on Vichy, helped Japan obtain a quota of her own from French Indo-China's rubber production. In return, Japanese assistance to Germany in the field of transportation was forthcoming. While their own immediate wartime needs kept the allies from pushing matters to the breaking point, the issue of principle was finally settled only in 1943 in the context of a comprehensive economic treaty designed to regulate relations between the European and Far Eastern Axis spheres. Germany then recognized that in the future the treaties of one signatory with an independent country in the sphere of another signatory could be concluded only after consultation with the power exercising "leadership" over that sphere.[15] In spite of its formally bilateral character, this stipulation was a one-sided victory for the Japanese. As a German memorandum of the spring of 1941 had pointed out, Germany stood to lose much more than Japan from such an arrangement because her economic stake in the Far East and Southeast Asia was incomparably greater than Japan's in Europe or Africa.

While Germany could easily agree to Japan's political leadership of Indo-China and less easily, but eventually, to her economic dominance as well, many

Germans found it hard to swallow Japan's claim to the Dutch East Indies. The political status of the Dutch colony differed sharply, of course, from that of Indo-China. The Dutch East Indies owed allegiance to the Dutch Government-in-Exile and not to a regime subject to German pressure. This made matters easier for the Japanese, since Germany was unlikely to obtain the kinds of economic advantage in the Indies which her control over Vichy helped her secure in Indo-China. On the other hand, Japan was less likely to obtain from the Dutch government in London or from Batavia the concessions which Vichy and Saigon, in part under German pressure, had made in order to facilitate Japan's political and military infiltration of the French colony.

In the German view, however, the conquest of the Netherlands had brought Germany a kind of right of control over the Dutch East Indies. The German position, though never hardened enough to make the issue critical, was interesting in that it contradicted Germany's concession of political control to Japan in the negotiations of September 1940, not to mention the German declaration of disinterestedness in the Indies in May of that year.

Shortly after the defeat of Holland, the German Foreign Ministry demanded that Japan break off relations with the Dutch government in London and conduct all her relations with Holland and the Dutch East Indies through Berlin. The Japanese complied only in part. They continued relations with the Dutch Government-in-Exile but professed to consider the Dutch minister in Tokyo as the spokesman for Batavia, with which they were determined to negotiate independently of Berlin about Japanese interests in the Indies. Germany at the same time conceded that

Japan might settle technical and minor economic matters in direct talks with Batavia.[16]

While the German foreign office agreed to this face-saving arrangement and did its best in late July 1940 not to alarm the Japanese with the prospect of a German-controlled Dutch East Indies, Hitler himself seems to have favored an arrangement whereby Holland would obtain a formally autonomous status in the new Europe to enable her to hold on to her Asian possessions. He expressed himself in this vein to his entourage in June, and as late as August 1940 Arthur Seyss-Inquart was permitted to develop similar plans in the Nazi party organ, *Monatshefte für auswärtige Politik.*[17]

More surprising than this cleavage between party and diplomatic circles in matters of tactics is the fact that neither the German declaration of May 1940 of disinterestedness in the Indies nor the clauses of the Tripartite Pact were viewed by the German government as an abandonment of its rightful claim to supervise the colonial affairs of its Dutch ward. Hitler told Mussolini on October 4, 1940, that in the New European Order, "the Netherlands should remain independent, if only because of their colonies"[18] —this a week after the German negotiators in Tokyo had agreed to Japan's leadership over the Dutch East Indies. The state secretary in the foreign ministry expressed much the same thought six weeks later.[19] When Germany tried, during the winter and spring of 1940–1941, to induce Japan to attack Singapore, high military and civilian officials in Berlin still thought that a German renunciation of claims to the Dutch East Indies or to the former German islands in the Pacific could be held out to Japan as bait.[20] We will never know how the Japanese would have responded to the offer of a reward they already considered theirs, because Ribbentrop was eventually persuaded not to raise the issue in his talks with Matsuoka in the spring of 1941. The advice, incidentally, had come from Stahmer, signer of the secret addenda, who seemed determined to keep them forever secret from Ribbentrop.[21]

The issue of the Dutch East Indies turned up once more in German-Japanese relations in 1942, when the Japanese occupied the Dutch colony. Counsels in Berlin were again divided. Members of the German administration in Holland were under strong pressure from the leader of the Dutch Nazi movement, Anton Mussert, to protect at least the interests and the activities of Mussert's followers in the Indies; this view had some support in the foreign ministry. But the embassy in Tokyo and eventually the foreign minister himself realized that Japanese suspicions would be rekindled if Germany tried to protect any Dutch interests in the Indies;[22] between Japan and Mussert, the German preference was clear. For similar reasons, the German government in January 1942 vetoed attempts by private German individuals to purchase properties in the Indies from Dutchmen in Holland, in an effort to preserve them from expropriation by the Japanese.[23] From February 1942 on, the Dutch in Holland were told by the German authorities to write off their colonial empire.[24]

THE GERMAN STAKE IN GREATER EAST ASIA

Of larger significance in the long run than any individual colony of the old imperialist powers would be the role that European business would be allowed in the new Japanese empire, the Greater East Asia Co-Prosperity Sphere. The biggest bone of contention between Germany and Japan was the status of German business in China and Manchuria. Would Japan, for instance, spare Germany from the systematic harassment to which she subjected the commercial interests of other European nations in China? Berlin was concerned in this matter not merely for the sake of prestige, but because Germany in the twentieth century had developed a substantial trade in China. Despite the loss of her privileged status in China under the Versailles treaty, Germany had built up an impressive market in the 1920s and 1930s, which provided a valuable outlet for her manufactured products and a source of precious raw materials.

Along with other Western businessmen, the Germans had suffered from the repercussions of the China Incident and the Japanese attempt to monopolize Chinese trade in her own interest. When the German government threw its support behind Japanese policy in China in the spring of 1938 by canceling contracts for war material with Chiang Kai-shek and recalling the German military advisers to the Nationalist government, it confidently expected to be rewarded by economic privileges in the provinces occupied by Japan. These hopes were quickly disappointed as Ribbentrop through 1938 and 1939 unsuccessfully strove for some recognition of a preferential status for German interests in China, as compared to those of other Western powers.[25]

At the time of the negotiations for a tripartite treaty Germany made another attempt to obtain a written guarantee from Japan for German preferential status in China. Again, the Japanese refused.[26] Undaunted, the Germans renewed their efforts in early 1941. This time Japanese requests for German aid in the fields of heavy industry and war technology had led to the dispatch of a German economic mission to Tokyo. This, the Germans thought, created a favorable atmosphere in which to renew German requests concerning China. It had become clear by the time the German economic mission set out for Japan in March 1941 that its negotiations would cover the whole range of economic questions between the two powers and their respective spheres. The interests of German business in China were a chief concern to the German negotiators.

The negotiations between the German mission headed by Dr. H. Wohlthat and the Japanese took far longer than either side had expected; both parties used whatever bargaining power they had over immediate and pressing issues in order to shape the long-term agreement which had been the original aim of the Wohlthat mission. Japan used her control over the raw materials of East and Southeast Asia, Germany her armaments and technical aid.

The treaty text which was published in January 1943 was meant for popular consumption and hardly touched on the real issues which had made agreement so hard to reach. The core of the bargain lay hidden in two secret annexes to the treaty, signed in Berlin along with the official treaty text, and a number of secret additional protocols signed in Tokyo. Together, the documents constituted a compromise of the initial objectives of the two parties, with the advantage perhaps slightly on the Japanese side. In addition, the documents gave a general insight into the kind of economic New Orders that the Axis powers might have established in the event of a Tripartite victory.

The Germans had to concede to the Japanese that

their relations with countries in Greater East Asia would in the future be conducted only in consultation with Japan. This was a blow to German business in Southeast Asia and China. On the other hand, the Germans finally secured a written guarantee of preferential treatment in Greater East Asia as compared to third powers (Articles Four and Seven of the first secret protocol). The victory which had eluded them so long was marred, however, by the additional stipulation that military necessity would release Japan from strict observation of this principle. No doubt Japanese needs and Germany's ability to pressure Japan—not the treaty clauses—would have determined the future shape of Nazi German business in a Japanese-controlled Asia.

Finally, the economic agreements attempted to do what the Tripartite Pact had overlooked: define the exact limits of the "spheres" of the two powers. Though it was not a definitive statement of the borders of the New Orders, the first secret addendum to the Berlin treaty of January 1943 roughly defined the New Orders as the areas effectively under German and Japanese occupation. India was thus not included in the Japanese sphere, nor were Australia and New Zealand, but future claims to such domination were still possible. Nor did Germany claim all of Europe as her *Wirtschaftsraum,* but limited the applicability of the economic treaties to the areas already annexed to the Reich and the areas actually occupied by German troops.

Although the stipulations concerning the future economic role of one signatory in the sphere of the other were formally reciprocal, both Germany and Japan realized that the relevant clauses had a greater bearing on European rights in East Asia than on Japanese interests in Europe. This was partly because Germany's economic stake in Greater East Asia was considerably larger than Japan's in Europe, but also because other European nations had far greater interests in East Asia than Asian countries had in Europe and the treaties of January 1943 were likely to set the pattern not only for German-Japanese economic relations but for the future relationship of a German-dominated Europe with a Japanese-dominated Asia. Still, the ticklish question of what would happen to the economic interests and rights of other European powers in East Asia was left untouched by the treaties. Presumably, the fate of these nations would vary with the kind of political bond that united any particular European country with Germany, official spokesman in the eyes of the Japanese for all European interests.

A PLACE FOR LESSER ARYANS

Among nations thus ranked in the German New Order, Italy, co-equal with her two partners in the Tripartite Pact, stood highest, and, in fact, Japan concluded with her an economic agreement along the lines of the Japanese-German treaty, actually signing in Berlin and Rome on the same day. Economically, the whole question was less important for Italy than for Germany, since Italy's market in China and the Far East in general was small compared to Germany's. On the other hand, as a victor in World War One and a participant in the Washington Conference of 1921–1922, Italy enjoyed preferential rights in China superior to Germany's. Juridically, therefore, Italy had more to lose in the Far East by recognizing Japan's hegemony, since as late as January 1943 Italy still enjoyed extraterritorality in

China, in addition to some of the other appurtenances of Western imperialism, such as a concession in Tientsin and, under the Boxer protocol, the right to station forces in Peking and in Chinese waters.

Shortly after the conclusion of the economic treaties, including the grant of Italian preferential status in China, Nippon divested Italy of all of her treaty rights in China. Ostensibly, this took the form of a Japanese request to Italy to retrocede to Nanking the treaty rights Italy was enjoying in China. This gesture toward her own puppet, Japan averred, was to coincide with Wang Ching-wei's declaration of war against the Western powers. More probably, Japan wanted the Tripartite powers to match the British and American surrender of their old treaty rights to *their* wartime ally, Chungking. Italy conceded, and on February 14, 1943, she surrendered her treaty rights to the Nanking regime.[27] Whether the Germans exercised the pressure on Rome for which Japan had asked is not known. No doubt the conclusion of the January agreements had softened the blow for Italy.

France, within the German New Order by defeat, was less fortunate. Not a member of the Tripartite Pact, she could not expect to benefit from the economic privileges which the Tripartite powers granted each other. Yet when she was asked by Tokyo to surrender her treaty rights and concessions, including the French naval base at Kwangchouwan, to Nanking, she put up more resistance than did Italy. In the end, though, France too acceded, and in part under German pressure.[28] By an exchange of letters between the French governor-general in Indo-China and the Japanese envoy in Saigon, France on February 16, 1943, gave up extraterritoriality in China and retroceded her concessions in Shanghai, Tientsin,

Hankow, and Canton. At the same time, a Franco-Japanese agreement provided for the Japanese occupation of Kwangchouwan. Here, not even the pretense of strengthening Nanking's morale or rewarding her declaration of war against Britain and the United States (January 9, 1943) was maintained, and the Japanese did not hesitate to succeed openly to French treaty rights in China. Only in March 1945 did the Japanese premier offer Kwangchouwan to the Nanking government.[29]

German domination of Europe did not work everywhere to the disadvantage of the old European colonial powers. While Germany on some occasions assisted the demise of European colonialism in Asia, at other times she helped European countries to preserve their colonial holdings within Greater East Asia. Portugal is one example. The Germans were anxious that Portugal maintain her neutrality, thus denying the Allies the use of the Azores or Madeira as a base against "Fortress Europe"; Berlin did its best to smooth Portuguese-Japanese relations in the Far East in order to prevent Portugal from joining the enemy coalition through the back door in Asia. Japan indeed left Macao intact as the only European colony along the China coast and exercised sufficient restraint during her occupation of Portuguese Timor to prevent an open rupture with Lisbon. Japan was in part motivated by a desire for Brazil's continued neutrality, but there is some evidence that consideration for her German ally played some role in shaping Japan's policies toward Portugal and her possessions in Asia.[30]

A similar condition prevailed with respect to the political status of French Indo-China. Again, Japan had reasons of her own for valuing the existence of a smoothly functioning, yet politically obedient, colonial administration in Indo-China. But her formal respect for the French regime and French sovereignty was at least partly motivated during 1941 and 1942 by her consideration for the recurrent German desire for a rapprochement with Vichy.[31] Before the end of the Second World War, however, Japan had turned from benefactor to beneficiary of the Franco-German relationship. When Allied landings in French North Africa and the German occupation of the remainder of France threatened to ruin Berlin's relations with Vichy in November 1942, it was the Japanese who worried about the untoward consequences which a break between Vichy and Berlin might have on the pliable and useful regime in Saigon.[32]

THE SECOND PARTITION OF ASIA

The Tripartite Pact had not defined the precise limits of the signatories' New Orders nor had it determined the future status of large areas of the world. The need to regulate their economic relations, even in wartime, had forced the Tripartite powers to give greater precision to the boundaries of their New Orders and to the concept of "leadership" which had been enshrined in the Tripartite Pact without definition. Similarly, the military developments of the war raised the question of the future organization and domination of the areas which lay between the spheres of the European and the Far Eastern Axis powers. This intervening area comprised all the territory of the Soviet Union in the north; in the south it included the whole arc in which British influence predominated, from the Arabian peninsula in the west to India in the east. At the time of the conclusion of the Tripartite Pact, Germany and Japan had assumed that, in case Russia joined their alliance, Russian expansion toward the Persian Gulf and India would be encouraged, or at any rate tolerated.[33] After the German attack on Russia, there was no further reason, at least in Berlin, to "reserve" southwestern Asia for the expansion of the Soviet Union. And after Pearl Harbor and the Japanese entry into the war against England, there were additional military reasons for dividing the intervening space among the Tripartite powers. If military operations by the three powers were to be conducted in this area to overthrow the British position at its weakest point, operational limits for the campaigns would have to be established. Eventually, Germany and Japan would wish to succeed Britain as the dominant power in the area, and a political delimitation of their respective spheres of influence or of permanent occupation would have to be agreed upon.

The Japanese were the first to approach the question with frankness and in detail. Their draft for a military convention with Germany and Italy, presented in Berlin on December 15, 1941, contained a division of the Indian Ocean and the areas bordering it to the north into a German-Italian and a Japanese operational zone.[34] The Japanese treaty draft fixed the dividing line along the 70th degree eastern longitude. Ostensibly, this was a strictly technical, narrowly military line, which would, moreover, apply in practice largely to the three powers' naval activities in the Indian Ocean and not to operations on land. The 70th degree, as can be seen from the map on page 111, cuts through the Indian Ocean some 1000 miles east of Madagascar and the eastern tip of Africa. Farther north, it enters the Indian subcontinent near the mouth of the Indus River and then cuts north through British India and the eastern part of Afghanistan into Soviet territory. It follows a line through the Soviet Union approximately 600 miles east of the Ural mountains.

While the German authorities, both civilian and military, disliked the 70th degree line, they did so for different reasons and they proposed different alternatives. The foreign ministry and the military saw the proposed line as an attempt to fix future political frontiers, but while the navy accepted such a future delimitation, the diplomats objected, especially to the idea that virtually all of India would be incorporated in Greater East Asia.[35] The navy, and in the end OKW, agreed to sign the Japanese proposal, insisting orally to the Japanese that the 70th degree line would have to be treated flexibly in case either power operated in its vicinity in the Indian Ocean.[36] Within OKW, certain agencies were opposed to the Japanese draft, which they thought might handicap their future control and exploitation of the Soviet Union. Their alternative is contained in a draft by the Office of War Economy and Armaments (*Wehrwirtschafts- und Rüstungsamt*), a branch of OKW, which received the implicit sanction of its parent authority.[37] The Office was ready to assign all of India to the Japanese sphere, adding Afghanistan for good measure. It wanted the German-Japanese dividing line to follow existing international boundaries rather than to cut through existing states. For that very reason, and on geographic grounds, as the Office maintained, the German-Japanese dividing line on the continent of Asia should rather follow the Persian-Indian and then the Persian-Afghan border; it was then to turn sharply eastward, following the Russo-Afghan, Russo-Indian, and Russo-Chinese borders (Sinkiang being

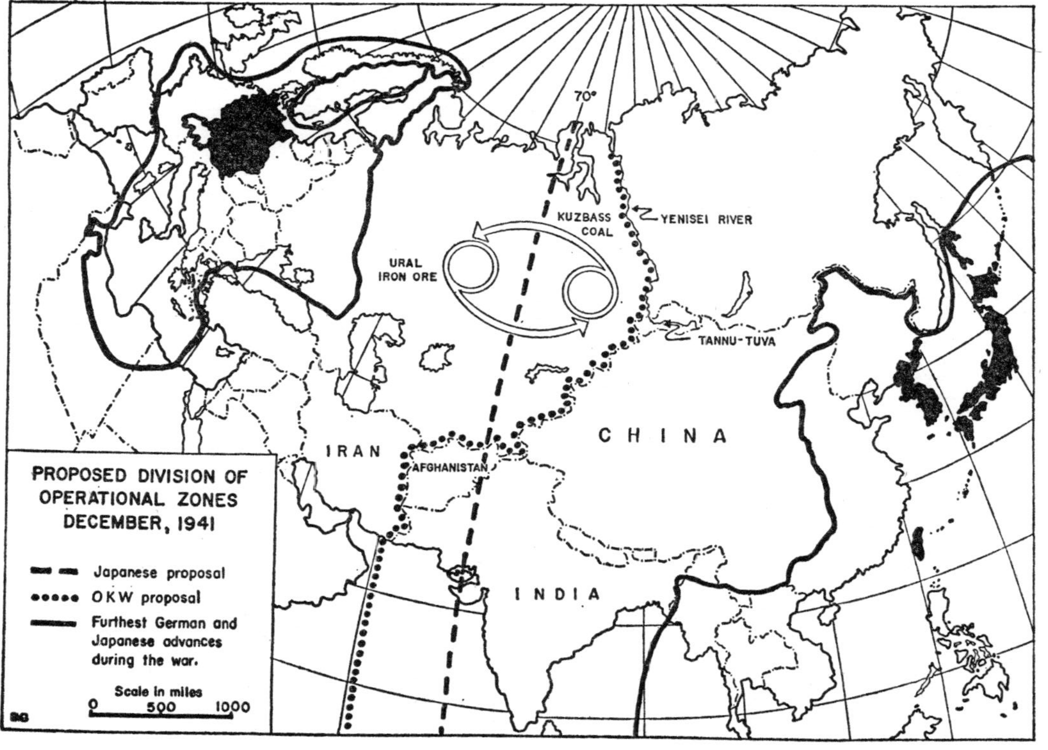
PROPOSED DIVISION OF
OPERATIONAL ZONES
DECEMBER, 1941
Japanese proposal
OKW proposal
Furthest German and
Japanese advances
during the war.
Scale in miles
0 500 1000
70°
KUZBASS
COAL
YENISEI RIVER
URAL
IRON ORE
TANNU-TUVA
IRAN
AFGHANISTAN
CHINA
INDIA

recognized as a part of China). The dividing line eventually was to follow the border between the Soviet Union and Tannu Tuva and then turn sharply north to follow the Yenisei River into the Arctic Ocean.

The map on page 111 contrasts the original Japanese proposal and the line advocated by the Office of War Economy and Armaments. It also suggests what may have been the basic reason for the Office's advocacy of the strangely S-shaped line through Asia: by insisting that *its* boundary line had the advantage of leaving "economically integrated" areas intact, the Office meant to indicate that Germany, under the German proposal, would secure both the iron ore of the Ural Mountains and the coal of the Kuznetsk Basin, areas already integrated under successive Soviet Five-Year Plans, which the 70th degree line would have divided.

While the records of German internal deliberations give the historian some insight into Berlin's ultimate objectives, the German government decided not to take the Japanese into its confidence concerning its territorial ambitions in the Soviet Union. It was thought that specific revisions of the proposed line would only arouse Japanese suspicion. The question of carving up the Soviet Union was at any rate premature as long as Japan remained at peace with Russia. The German government therefore decided to sign the Japanese draft without major revisions. The 70th degree line was accepted as the dividing line of the respective operational spheres in the Indian Ocean, with the addition of the word "approximately," inserted before "70th degree" in order to insure sufficient flexibility for naval operations, especially for the German auxiliary cruisers which had operated in the Indian Ocean for some time. In addition, the chief of OKW, General Wilhelm Keitel, who signed the military convention in January 1942 on behalf of Germany, informed the Japanese representatives orally after the signing that the dividing line was not to be considered as a political boundary and that operational zones on the continent of Asia (that is, in Russia) could only be decided upon "once the question had become acute," an obvious reference to the Japanese entry into the war against Russia.[38]

In regard to India, too, the Germans thought it unwise to press for any modification of the Japanese proposal. As Ribbentrop explained:

> If Germany should reject the 70th degree longitude because it assigns British India to the Japanese sphere, this would arouse the suspicion of the Japanese government. On the contrary, it is in our interest to see Japan stake out the furthest possible military and territorial claims in East Asia and to engage Great Britain decisively in that area. This is the best antidote against a possible military inactivity there on the part of Japan once she has reached her nearest goals, and against possible British efforts to drive a wedge between Japan and ourselves.[39]

The German decision to subordinate her own territorial and economic interests in Asia to the military demands of the moment was undoubtedly wise. Even so, the conflict between her immediate military demands, which required a strong Japanese presence in the western Indian Ocean, and her long-term political interests in that area, which forbade recognizing India as part of the Greater East Asia Sphere, continued to preoccupy the European Axis leaders during the spring of 1942.

Through February and March, as the Japanese approached the Indian border, Germany looked askance at the westward expansion of her ally's claim to rule. Ambassador Ott reported from Tokyo on the "geographically and politically unwarranted interpretation of the Greater East Asia Sphere" by the Japanese press, which, he reported, now annexed India as well as Australia and New Zealand to that sphere; despite Berlin's instructions to proceed with caution, he warned the Japanese that Germany too was interested in Indian affairs.[40] Italy viewed the westward extension of Greater East Asia with even greater alarm than did her German ally, either because she considered her own "sphere" in eastern and northeastern Africa endangered by Japanese claims to India, or because, as a European colonial power, she was particularly sensitive to the damage which Japanese claims might inflict upon the notion of Europe's civilizing mission among colonial peoples.

Notwithstanding these signs of alarm in Rome as well as in the German embassy in Tokyo, the German Foreign Ministry adhered to its decision of January not to query the Japanese about the westward extension of their sphere. References to the "yellow peril" were removed from German publications by the censors of the foreign ministry.[41] The Japanese must have thought along similar lines, for they too refused to risk a quarrel with their allies over territory which neither of them had as yet conquered. In early April, Tokyo invited Berlin and Rome to cosponsor a declaration of Indian independence, indicating at least implicitly that Japan recognized the rights of Germany and Italy to be heard on Indian affairs.[42] Similarly, propaganda, intelligence, and subversive activities against British rule in India were to some extent coordinated by the three powers, often at Japanese initiative.[43]

As a matter of fact, however, Germany for a time had a somewhat more advantageous position than Japan as sponsor of an Indian-led independence movement. Although Japan had captured in Singapore many Indian soldiers whom she tried to fashion into a Japanese-controlled Indian Liberation Army during the summer of 1942, the Germans down to 1943 held a superior drawing card in the person of Subhas Chandra Bose, easily the most attractive figure among Indian leaders seeking Tripartite support. Bose had come to Berlin, through Afghanistan and the Soviet Union, in early 1941 and had been encouraged to recruit Indian supporters in Europe. He was authorized to set up Indian troop formations in Europe, presumably with the idea of using them in India once Germany had crossed the Caucasus and stood ready to enter India.[44]

For a time, it looked as if Germany was going to use Bose's presence in Europe in order to strengthen her own position in India vis-à-vis Japan, just as the Indian leader requested German support for his independence movement in part to counter too great a dependence on the Japanese.[45] But in the end the Germans once more decided to subordinate their own interest in India to the more immediate requirement of weakening the British. They did not object in early 1943 to Bose's departure for Asia, where Japan's presence on the very borders of India seemed to present the Indian leader with a more promising field of activity than his radio station in Berlin afforded him. In fact, a German and a Japanese submarine cooperated in bringing Bose to East Asia.[46]

Eventually, the course of military operations assured that the German-Japanese alliance would not be shattered by a fight over the spoils of war in the Indian subcontinent.

As with India, the fate of the Arab-speaking areas of southwestern Asia had not been definitely decided between the Tripartite powers in 1940. "Arabia," as it was sometimes called in Tripartite propaganda declarations, was assigned neither to the European nor to the Asian New Order. Indeed, the tacit agreement of Berlin and Tokyo not to quarrel over as yet unconquered areas seems to have worked as well as it did largely because Japan's recognition of Germany's right to participate in all basic dispositions concerning India was matched by Germany's readiness to let Japan be heard on Arab affairs. Perhaps this arrangement was already foreshadowed in the military convention of January 1942, which, by assigning to Germany a slice of India and to Japan a slice of Afghanistan, gave the Germans a foothold in India and the Japanese one in the Middle East. It is very likely, too, that Germany welcomed some Japanese influence in the Middle East to offset in part Italian claims of hegemony in that area.[47]

JAPAN AND THE GERMAN NEW ORDER

German-Japanese negotiations on territorial matters dealt almost exclusively with the status of German and European rights in Greater East Asia, or with the future of the areas which separated the German-Italian New Order from the Japanese. By comparison, Japanese interests in the German-Italian sphere received little attention. In the deliberations preceding the arrival of Minister Stahmer in Tokyo in early September 1940, the Japanese had been ready to recognize a German-Italian sphere in Europe *and* Africa. But as the discussions progressed in Tokyo and the German negotiators did not insist on the inclusion of Africa in the German sphere, in the end the Tripartite Pact merely referred to a New Order in Europe. Even so, the Japanese probably continued to be ready to recognize any claims that Germany chose to assert over territory in Africa. Her suggestion of the 70th degree line, and her views about Madagascar in the spring of 1942, leave little doubt that Japan considered Africa safely within the German-Italian sphere.

The issue became of interest in the early spring of 1942 when the spectacular Japanese victories in Southeast Asia raised the possibility of a Japanese advance into the western Indian Ocean, including the acquisition of bases in Madagascar. It is not certain whether it was the Japanese who first broached the question of Madagascar in Berlin or whether the Germans suspected Japanese designs on the island before Tokyo had raised the issue. The first German reference to the matter occurred as early as December 22, 1941, in the war diary of the German naval staff. The naval staff discussed Japan's intention, recently disclosed, of securing [*sich aneignen*] bases on Madagascar. The naval staff favored such a step on purely military grounds but thought that political objections —the unfavorable effect on the German-French relationship and the "extension of the yellow sphere of influence far beyond the 70th degree to the west"— so far outweighed the military advantage that "it appears right to work consciously against this Japanese intention."

Nothing more was heard of the matter for almost two months. But shortly after the conquest of Singapore on February 15, 1942, Japanese naval officers in Tokyo informally indicated to the German naval attaché their strong interest in bases on Madagascar. They explained that they expected to secure them with the assent of Vichy. Ambassador Ott asked for instructions in the matter of Madagascar, since he expected the Japanese to raise the issue formally almost any day.[48]

The German Foreign Ministry was lukewarm at first, though not as hostile as the navy had been in December. On February 27, it instructed Ott not to raise the matter of Madagascar on his own initiative but to report all Japanese overtures to Berlin. For his own information, the ambassador was told that a Japanese occupation of the island would be welcome on military grounds as long as Japan asked for the Reich's approval of such a westward extension of her operations sphere. There might be political objections to a Japanese hold on Madagascar, Ott was told, but the foreign ministry refused to spell them out or to assess their weight in comparison with the military benefits of the operation, which it had admitted.[49]

The foreign ministry's chief objection referred to the untoward consequences which the Japanese occupation of Madagascar might have on German-French relations. For that reason, the German navy, by the spring an ardent supporter of a Japanese landing on Madagascar, urged the foreign ministry and OKW in early March to submit the whole matter to the French and to remove French objections to the proposed Japanese action at once.[50]

Whether the German government acted on the navy's suggestion is not known. Perhaps the Japanese had already approached Vichy on their own before

Berlin found time to take the matter up with the French; the French government at any rate thought it necessary in early March to deny that it was negotiating with Tokyo about a Japanese occupation of Madagascar.[51]

Most likely, the Germans hesitated through the middle of March. When Admiral Raeder reported the Japanese request for bases on Madagascar to Hitler on March 12, the Führer showed little interest in the project. While Raeder spoke of the important effects which such a step might have on German-French relations, Hitler thought that the whole matter would take care of itself since "France [would] not give her consent."[52] Evidently, he did not consider the operation important enough to exert his own considerable influence over Vichy in its favor.

Whether Hitler changed his mind soon afterward or whether Ribbentrop spoke without the Führer's approval when he saw Oshima shortly thereafter is not certain. But the foreign minister came out in favor of a Japanese occupation of the French island, provided the necessary political guarantees were given to Germany. In the words of Ribbentrop:

> the Japanese advance into the Indian Ocean might raise the question of Madagascar. Madagascar belonged to our European-African sphere of interest and had to remain in it. We also desired that it remain with France, but we would, under certain circumstances, agree to it that Japan obtain naval and air bases in Madagascar for the duration of the war. I [Ribbentrop] therefore asked Oshima to inquire of his government whether Japan planned any action against Madagascar. If so, we assumed that Japan agreed to our views as stated above to the effect that Madagascar belonged to our sphere of interest and that she would be ready

to give assurances to us as well as to the French government that Japanese forces would evacuate Madagascar after the end of the war. The fact of this exchange of opinions concerning Madagascar would have to be kept absolutely secret, needless to say. If necessary, Germany was ready, in case Japan planned any action against Madagascar, to help smooth the way in Vichy [*zur Applanierung der Situation in Vichy beitragen*].[53]

Ribbentrop went over the same ground with Oshima on March 23, which indicates that no reply from Tokyo had then been received. Indeed, after the middle of March, Japanese interest in the Madagascar operation waned, if it had ever been as strong as the Germans surmised and at times feared. No further German-Japanese exchanges in the matter have been discovered.

Instead, the French by late April approached the Japanese in the matter. They now anticipated an English landing on the island and hoped to secure Japanese aid in its defense. Whether Germany had given her blessing to these Franco-Japanese exchanges and whether she had in fact pursued the matter of the evacuation guarantee is not known. In any case, nothing came of the French effort to salvage Madagascar for the Vichy regime with Japanese help. On May 5, British units landed on the island, and although Franco-Japanese conversations concerning Japanese aid to the hard-pressed French defenders continued for some days at least, no Japanese help was forthcoming.[54]

The danger of an imminent Japanese invasion, by which the British had justified their own landings before world opinion, would seem to have been greatly exaggerated. Only some Japanese midget submarines landed their crews on Madagascar, and they arrived after the British landings. It is possible that the Japanese, who were quickly apprehended and executed, had made use of some of the German maps and data concerning Madagascar which Japan had requested and obtained from the German navy in early May.[55]

Aside from Madagascar, no other issue forced the Germans to choose between their immediate military needs and their ultimate political objectives within their own sphere. Japan had no military plans which involved operations in the German-Italian sphere, and her political and economic relations with the countries in the new Europe developed smoothly enough. Loyalty to the Tripartite Pact required that Japan withdraw diplomatic recognition from governments defeated by the Reich—particularly those governments which had moved into exile in Britain. As we have seen, Holland presented a rather special case, and Japan continued to recognize the Dutch Government-in-Exile in London until the outbreak of the Pacific war. Even in the case of the Polish Government-in-Exile, she was remarkably late in breaking diplomatic relations. Not until October 1941 did Japan withdraw recognition from the Polish government in London,[56] ratifying the "extinction" of Poland in the spirit of the Tripartite Pact.

Similarly, Japan was expected to honor with diplomatic recognition those German satellites which were permitted formal independence (Slovakia, Croatia, Republic of Salò). In all, Japan maintained a sizable number of diplomatic missions in German-dominated Europe. These missions and those in neutral European countries and in Vichy served Japan well as listening posts and provided Tokyo with more balanced reporting about the European war than was usually forthcoming from the embassy in Berlin. In 1943 and

1944 many of these Japanese legations were involved in negotiations for a separate German-Soviet truce and, after the collapse of the Reich, in overtures to the Western powers looking toward a negotiated surrender to the Allies.

Having recognized the German New Order and many of its constituent members, Japan was not expected to offer advice on the political shape of Nazi Europe. Yet she had to realize that Germany's political demands often stood in the way of winning a war in which Japan too was vitally interested. From mid-1942 on, and especially in 1943, Japanese diplomats suggested that greater autonomy be given to the small states of Europe. They found a more sympathetic hearing in Rome than in Berlin.[57] When the Japanese took their advice directly to Berlin, they sometimes suggested autonomy for the Russian borderlands.[58] While some members of the German government sympathized with the Japanese views, it was official policy not to heed the Japanese point, but to brush it aside curtly. Ribbentrop did so with the remark that, contrary to Japanese claims, the Ukraine could not be compared with Burma.[59] Finally discouraged, the Japanese abandoned their efforts after 1944. Each Axis power was now free to make its own political mistakes in the sphere which was at least not contested by its ally.

On balance, the powers' conduct in regard to territorial matters shows more good sense and rationality than most other aspects of their relationship. While each power's claim to a New Order was inspired by unrealistic dreams of grandeur, in their relations with each other Germany and Japan knew well how to subordinate marginal territorial issues to more immediate needs. Where intensive bickering or bargaining occurred, it was over concrete economic issues, seldom over matters of prestige or face. True, greater Axis military successes, especially beyond the borders of the original spheres, might well have led to intense territorial conflict. But if Germany and Japan failed to achieve a satisfactory coordination of their respective diplomatic and military policies, it was not because of conflicting designs for a new division of the world.

ing occurred, it was over concrete economic issues, seldom over matters of prestige or face. True, greater Axis military successes, especially beyond the lines of the original spheres, might well have led to intense German-Japanese conflict. But if Germany and Japan failed to achieve a satisfactory coordination of their respective diplomatic and military policies, it was not because of conflicting designs for a new division of the world.

THE EXCHANGE OF STRATEGIC RESOURCES

4

One of the avowed war aims of the Axis powers was to fashion conquered lands and satellites into self-sufficient economic "spheres" that would serve the strategic and economic needs of each master race. During the Second World War, however, neither Germany nor Japan nor any of the wider areas they brought under their temporary control was fully self-sufficient in the raw materials and industrial techniques needed for modern warfare. Germany and her "sphere" were deficient in a large number of industrial raw materials, among which rubber and certain ferroalloys had been traditionally imported from East and Southeast Asia. Japan lacked raw materials and manufacturing skills, among them certain techniques—particularly in the chemical, machine-tool, and precision-instrument industries—which were available in Germany. The failure of the two powers to work out a satisfactory exchange, trading what they had for what they needed, is further proof of the weakness of their wartime alliance.

When the Second World War broke out in Europe, there existed no general program for economic or technological coordination between the two countries. The recent Russo-German pact had left the Japanese in no mood to collaborate. A general economic treaty, considered by the two countries for over a year and finally initialed in late July 1939, was suspended by the Japanese in early September in the wake of the political rupture between the two nations and because of the difficulty of conducting ordinary business transactions with German companies under wartime conditions.[1]

In the fall of 1939, the outbreak of the war in Europe naturally affected the German economy more decisively than it did the Japanese, because Germany's new status as a belligerent and the British blockade cut her off immediately from some of her most important overseas sources of imports. By contrast, Japan still had access to the American market and to the raw-material resources of Southeast Asia on which her war economy primarily depended. Her peacetime pattern of trade had been only slightly affected by the undeclared Sino-Japanese war and the recent (July 1939) American decision to cancel the Japanese-American trade treaty as of early 1940.

Germany therefore depended on Japan more than Japan did on her. In particular, the Germans expected Japan to defy the British blockade and to provide the Reich with materials produced both in the area which Japan controlled politically and militarily (Japan, Manchuria, and parts of China) and in other countries, primarily of Southeast Asia and South America, where Japan could act as a purchaser of German imports. Unfortunately for Berlin, the condition of the Japanese economy and the policy of her government during the period of the "phony war" made a defiance of the British blockade neither feasible nor desirable from the Japanese point of view. Japan's own dependence on the markets of the Empire and of other areas in part susceptible to British influence made it inopportune for her to risk British displeasure for the sake of Germany.[2]

Political considerations such as these were chiefly responsible for the limited amount of assistance which Japan lent the German war economy during the first few months of the war. Economic considerations also played a role, though smaller. Germany's cancellation of a number of Japanese orders for heavy equipment contracted before the outbreak of hostilities and heavy German commitments for the export of capital goods to the Soviet Union (in the wake of the German-Soviet pact) convinced the Japanese that they stood to obtain little from those sectors of German industry in which they were anxious to place their heaviest orders.[3]

A TRICKLE OF AID

To recount in detail the story of Germany's disappointment over inadequate Japanese assistance during the "phony war" would be tedious. It will be sufficient to mention a few of the areas in which Japanese aid fell sorely short of German expectations. One critical area for Germany was that of edible oils and fats, since domestic production provided only 60 per cent of the amount needed. Before the war, imports of soybeans and similar crops from Manchuria had played an important role in closing the German "fat gap" (*Fettlücke*). With the outbreak of the war, German imports dropped precipitately; during the "phony war" period, German soybean imports from Manchuria sank to about 4 per cent of their prewar level; during the second half of 1940, they climbed back to about 12 per cent of their prewar level, while during the first half of 1941 they approached only 30 per cent.[4]

The steep decline of German soybean imports was felt all the more bitterly in Berlin since ample means of transportation from Manchuria were available during the first twenty months of the Second World War. In fact, as early as September 1939, the Soviet Union had granted Germany a 50-per-cent reduction in freight rates for the shipment of soybeans over the Trans-Siberian Railroad. This favorable arrangement was renewed in the German-Soviet commercial treaties of early 1940 and early 1941 and continued in force down to the outbreak of the Russo-German war.[5] Against this background of Soviet cooperation, the Germans held the Japanese solely responsible for frustrating German bean imports from Manchukuo. Specifically, the Japanese were accused of succumbing to British pressure to cut bean exports to the Reich, and of having reduced the amounts available to Germany by their own increased purchase of Manchurian beans.[6] It is perhaps further evidence of an inability or failure of each country to imagine the point of view of the other, a weakness already noted more specifically earlier, that Germany ignored the hostility she had invited among the Japanese by her pact with Russia. Thus the German charges could well have been true, if curiously unimaginative. In any case, there is no doubt that Japanese exports to Germany from areas under her immediate control fell far below what Berlin had anticipated.

Germany fared hardly better with her hopes that she would benefit from Japanese purchases on her behalf in Southeast Asia and South America. Berlin was most interested in having Japan purchase rubber in Southeast Asia, tin in Malaya and South America, and a number of ferroalloys in China and Southeast Asia, without which German steel production was gravely handicapped. No specific import figures for the period of the "phony war" are available, but a study by OKW's Office for War Economy and Armament of September 1940 gives totals for Japan's purchases on behalf of Germany during the entire first year of World War Two.[7]

Rubber, for example, was one of the strategic commodities which Germany had previously imported largely from Asia. Despite the progress of her synthetic-rubber production, Germany was still dependent in 1939 on imports of natural rubber, because the synthetic needed an admixture of natural rubber and still met only a part of the German need.[8] The great hopes placed in Japan were once more disappointed, since Japan managed to purchase no more than 2800 tons of rubber on Germany's behalf, under 5 per cent of Germany's annual peacetime imports from Asia. The Germans therefore were very short of rubber during the first nine months of the war, particularly since German rubber stockpiles at the beginning had covered only a two-months supply. In June 1940 the situation eased considerably when large Dutch and French stocks of raw and manufactured rubber fell into German hands. By this time Japan also seemed to change her attitude toward the German war economy's needs.

The story of tin and tungsten is similar. With Japan's help, Germany was able to acquire during the first year of the war somewhat over 5 per cent of her prewar annual tin imports from Asia and somewhat less than 5 per cent of her prewar tungsten imports.

In some respects, however, the German shortages of tin and Far Eastern ferroalloys turned out to be less damaging to her war production than might be expected from the crude comparison of prewar and wartime import figures. For one thing, German stockpiles in almost all the nonferrous metals and ferroalloys were considerably larger than her rubber stockpiles at the outbreak of the war. Tin and tungsten reserves, for instance, were adequate for approximately one year and alternative supplies were available in Europe. Moreover, booty from the occupied countries and scrap drives at home made up in part for the imports which were no longer available.

Most significantly, however, technical ingenuity permitted the production of less highly alloyed steels with little loss in quality, which meant that, despite sharply curtailed imports, German steel production was never seriously hampered by a shortage of ferro-alloys.[9]

Since Japanese purchasing of the materials requested by Germany was still unhampered during the first twelve months of the war by the British policy of "control at source" (pre-emptive buying, etc.) which became so important after the autumn of 1940, and since Germany apparently made adequate supplies of currency available to Japan, the conclusion that Japan made fewer exertions on Germany's behalf than she might have made seems unavoidable. The heavy blow dealt to German-Japanese relations in August 1939 accounts for the very modest exertions which Japan made on behalf of her former friend during the opening months of the European war. The late summer of 1940 marks, here as elsewhere, a turning point in German-Japanese relations. While the German ambassador had spoken as late as the second half of April of "serious German displeasure [*Verstimmung*] caused by the inadequate economic support on the part of Japan,"[10] a mutually more advantageous though not always agreeable relation was worked out after the fall of 1940. The political rapprochement of the two powers, the acquisition of greater Japanese control over the resources of Indo-China, and the continued availability of overland communications through Siberia—all these three factors account for the more intensive economic relations between the Axis powers in the period from the autumn of 1940 to June 1941.

COOPERATION AND COMPETITION

In Indo-China, Germany could now purchase directly, since hostilities with France had ceased. In Thailand, the German purchasing organization had been improved since the beginning of the war. Even so, German raw-material purchases proved difficult and less rewarding than she had expected. Where the Reich had previously battled British blockade measures, she now found herself competing with Japan in those parts of Southeast Asia which were newly accessible to her. The amounts of the Indo-Chinese rubber harvest of 1940 which had not been sold at the time of the Franco-German armistice were quickly bought up by the Japanese and the Americans and eluded Germany. But with her close relations to Vichy, Germany could expect to obtain a sizable portion of the total 1941 harvest, estimated at some 70,000 tons. Although Germany had played a distinctly minor role in the Indo-Chinese rubber market before the war, she now concluded agreements with France (in September 1940 and January 1941) which allotted to her 25,000 tons of the anticipated 1941 production. A substantial share of the French quota of 18,000 tons was also promised to the Reich.[11] The German effort to secure such a considerable share of the 1941 harvest ran into immediate opposition from Japan, however. Japan's objections to the impropriety of direct Franco-German dispositions concerning Indo-China have already been mentioned. Yet Japan did not object for reasons of prestige alone. The allotments to Germany and France and the 25,000 tons assigned to the United States (in order to acquire badly needed dollars for the French colony) threatened to leave Japan with practically no rubber imports from Indo-China. Japan was by now feeling the effects of Britain's policy of "control at source," which was directed against both Germany and herself. With imports from Malaya and the Dutch East Indies curtailed, she competed more fiercely with the Reich for a share of Indo-Chinese rubber production.

In the end, and as a result more of competition in the market than of political agreement, both nations were remarkably successful in obtaining the share they had wanted. Germany secured for herself the whole 25,000 tons, out of which she had initially promised to satisfy Japanese demands, and Japan acquired almost that much, at the expense of the shipment initially intended for the United States. Despite the lack of any formal agreement, the situation seemed tolerable for both sides.

It might seem that the Japanese occupation of French Indo-China (the northern part in September 1940; the southern in July 1941), reducing the political influence Germany might exercise there via Vichy, should have added to the German-Japanese strain. But on balance Germany profited economically from the military hold which Japan, partly with German assistance, had established over the French colony. Without Japanese occupation, the British policy of pre-emptive buying, supported by the United States, would have greatly reduced the rubber quota available to the Germans. Instead, Japanese pressure on the French authorities in Indo-China probably explains the colony's failure to cooperate fully in British economic warfare—a cooperation initially promised by the French early in 1941.[12] In the absence of Japanese garrisons, a pro-de Gaullist uprising might have removed Indo-China completely from German influence.

Whatever the extent of Japan's indirect assistance to Germany by virtue of her military presence in Indo-China, her aid in matters of transportation during this phase of the war is beyond doubt. All the Indo-Chinese rubber that reached Germany via the Trans-Siberian Railroad during the first five months of 1941 (some 12,000 tons) had been transported from Indo-China to Manchuria in Japanese bottoms. Additional quantities had in fact been taken by Japanese vessels to Manchuria, where they could not be loaded because of the outbreak of the Russo-German war.

The German success in obtaining rubber, however, obviously owed much to a special combination in Indo-China. Neither a general plan nor Japanese determination to cooperate assured as much success with other materials, as the quest for nonferrous metals and ferroalloys showed. No German or Japanese figures are available and it is necessary to rely on Russian data for transshipments from the Far East. According to Stalin, the following commodities passed through the Soviet Union from the Far East in this period: 1,087 tons of tungsten ore (compared with a German annual prewar import of 9,000 tons from China alone); 587 tons of tin ore and 538 tons of tin (compared with prewar annual imports from China and the Dutch East Indies together of about 13,000 tons of ore); 260 tons of antimony ore and 42 tons of antimony (compared with a prewar annual import of about 2,600 tons of ore from China alone).[13] Again, as in the first year of the war, imports of these metals from the Far East satisfied only a fraction of Germany's annual needs. But for reasons already mentioned (and also because ferroalloys were made available by Spain, Russia, and Finland) Germany's failure to obtain more of these metals from East Asia did not restrict the German steel industry seriously.

Several factors will suggest why Japan's help in the procurement of these metals was not greater. Just when the Japanese became politically ready to aid the German war economy by purchases in third countries, the British shifted their blockade effort from control at sea to control at source. Pre-emptive buying in areas under British control and in the Dutch East Indies thus reduced the amounts Japan was able to import, and consequently to re-export to Germany. Since Germany's enemies considered her shortage in ferroalloys to be one of the chief bottlenecks in her war industry, their pre-emptive buying and export controls were particularly stringent and effective in the case of these metals.[14]

The areas which Japan controlled directly produced only a small share of the metals requested by Germany. Indo-China, partly subject to Japanese control and the main source of Germany's rubber imports during this phase of the economic war, produced few of the required metals in sufficient quantities. China's production of these metals, it is true, was more abundant than Indo-China's. Yet Japan's partial occupation of China was of relatively little use to her or her ally, since most of the tin and tungsten production took place in Free China where the whole output was under government control. There the amounts produced in 1940 and 1941 had been allotted to the Soviet Union and the United States, where they served as collateral for some of the loans Chungking had secured, particularly those from Washington.[15]

Furthermore, Japan herself was experiencing shortages in the very materials Germany requested her to purchase. This was due in part to the Allied policies already referred to, but also to the Japanese policy of stockpiling for a war which seemed to come ever closer. With limits on her own metal imports from China, the Dutch East Indies, the British colonies, and America, Japan reserved whatever amounts she could secure exclusively for her own needs. Japanese pressure on Saigon, for example, helped her acquire practically all of Indo-China's 1941 metal production for her own needs. When the Germans tried to obtain guarantees of delivery from the French, as they had for rubber, they were told that the disposition of metals was out of the hands of Vichy.[16] Finally, after July 1941, Japanese buying, both for Germany and for herself, was drastically reduced as a result of the American, British, and Dutch embargoes, and so was Japan's capacity to re-export strategic materials to the Reich.

By this time, however, an even more significant obstacle to German-Japanese economic exchanges had arisen with the closing of the Siberian overland route after June 22, 1941. Several of Hitler's advisers had tried to dissuade the Führer from the attack on the Soviet Union by calling attention to the serious economic consequences of the rupture of Germany's last overland connection with the Far East. But Hitler decided, as Keitel aptly phrased it, "not to let himself be influenced by these economic difficulties."[17] What was a minor consideration for the German leader proved to be for the British "the real turning point in the economic war."[18]

TRANSPORTATION PROBLEMS

Just as Germany began to make sure of her sources of supply—with the aid of a better purchasing organization in Southeast Asia established after Wohlthat's arrival in Tokyo in late April 1941—her road from the Far East was cut. As if to increase the irony, the supplies waiting for her at the end of the blocked road grew to enormous proportions after Pearl Harbor, when Japan put large quantities at Germany's disposal out of the stocks and supplies she had conquered in the south. German raw-material stocks accumulated in Far Eastern ports and warehouses to the point where insurance and storage charges became a real burden. By December 1941 total German stockpiles in the Far East amounted to about 90,000 tons; a considerable portion of this amount probably consisted of soybeans and other oil-producing substances and oils stockpiled in Japan proper or in Manchuria. From 1942 on, extensive German stocks of some of the Southeast Asian raw materials accumulated in Japanese and Malayan warehouses. In July 1942 the German purchasing mission in Tokyo reported to Berlin that Japan had put a total of 60,000 tons of rubber from the 1942 harvest at Germany's disposal. One thousand tons of tungsten had also been promised, though on the whole the procurement of tungsten still proved difficult even in Japanese-dominated Asia. In most other respects, German-Japanese competition for raw materials now gave way to an expansive generosity on the part of the Japanese, who had brought the produce of Malaya and the Dutch East Indies under their control and who, no doubt, also attempted to improve their own chances of obtaining German economic aid by making generous offers of raw materials.[19]

With transportation a critical need by early 1942 and an overland route out of the question, Germany had to consider the possibilities of shipping by sea. French shipping had aided in the transport of Indo-Chinese raw materials to Axis Europe in 1940 and 1941 but seems to have played no role after Pearl Harbor. Japan had suspended shipping to Europe after August 1940 and was unable or unwilling to put vessels at Germany's disposal for the purpose of blockade running. Germany therefore had to fall back on her own ships and a few that Italy made available. In addition, a number of German merchant ships had either been caught in Japan at the time the war broke out in Europe or had escaped to Japan from British and South American waters afterward. With that small fleet, the blockade was challenged.

German and Italian blockade-breakers operated during a total of four shipping seasons, one prior to the German-Russian war and the others in the three winter seasons that followed. For all practical purposes, blockade running was restricted to the period from October to March, when heavy fog and bad seas in the Atlantic, where interception was most effective, hindered the hunters more than the hunted.

Of the five ships that had started on their way to Europe before June 1941, three reached their destination.[20] During the 1941–1942 season, eleven ships in all were sent from the Far East to Europe. All took the route through the South Pacific and around Cape Horn, with remarkable success. Nine ships reached Europe safely, one was intercepted by American forces in the Atlantic and detained, and only one was sunk—by a German submarine by mistake.[21]

The departures from the Far East during the next shipping season were even more numerous, though the number remained behind earlier goals. Sixteen ships left the Far East, but only four reached Axis Europe. Among the other twelve, four returned to Japan or were recalled, two were sunk, and six scuttled themselves when they were intercepted by the Allied blockade. Most of these losses occurred in the North Atlantic or the Bay of Biscay when the ships had completed nine-tenths of their voyage. The route during the 1942–1943 shipping season was around the Cape of Good Hope, where Japanese control of the eastern Indian Ocean presumably gave the ships a certain measure of protection. The Allied occupation of North Africa after November 1942 and the consequent control of the sea approaches to southwestern Europe explained the drastic decline in successful blockade breaking from one year to the next. During the winter of 1943–1944, results were even more disastrous. Only five ships departed from the Far East, and only one of them reached Europe. Blockade breaking with surface vessels was therefore abandoned.[22]

In spite of the tremendous losses sustained, especially after late 1942, the blockade-runners had contributed much to the German war economy. During the four shipping seasons from 1940–1941 to 1943–1944, more than 200,000 tons of cargo were sent to Germany from East and Southeast Asia and over half of it reached the Reich. Of that half, 44,000 tons were rubber, over 50,000 tons edible oils and fats, over 6000 tons metals and ores (an exact breakdown is not available), and the remainder minor quantities of mica, quinine, wood oil, tea, etc.[23]

The heavy losses of the 1942–1943 season had already turned the German government's attention to the possibility of blockade breaking by submarine. In January 1943, Hitler gave orders to build special cargo submarines with a loading capacity of 500 tons. Twenty boats were scheduled to be completed by mid-1944, after which, it was estimated, Germany might count on them to ship 20,000 tons from the Far East annually (20 boats times 2 annual trips times 500 tons).[24] In the meantime, standard submarines with a very much smaller loading capacity (seldom much over 200 tons) had to be put in operation. The Italians, who had contributed four surface vessels to run the blockade, now made a number of submarines available. The Japanese, too, were prevailed upon during the latter part of 1943 to participate with two submarines in the blockade-running program.[25]

Despite the apparent superiority of submarines on some counts—their ability to escape detection and sail year round—they fared badly. Allied radar had made such progress by the time the submarine program got under way in the second half of 1943 that the losses were almost as heavy as were those of the surface vessels. A large number of boats were lost on the way to the Far East. Many others could not make the return journey because of damages sustained en route or the need for extensive repairs. Of the twelve submarines that left Japan for Europe, only four reached their destination. Of the two Japanese submarines, only one reached Europe, and it was lost on the return voyage.[26]

The results of the submarine transport program, if measured in bulk alone, can hardly have been large. The maximum cargo that could have reached Europe on the five boats which made the trip safely may have been around 1000 tons. To judge from the loading schedule of one of the boats, most of this tonnage must have consisted of rubber, with some tungsten and small amounts of quinine and opium.[27]

JAPAN FORMULATES HER DEMANDS

Germany's aid to Japan differed only in kind, not in spirit, from Japan's to Germany. While Japanese requests were presented in Berlin as urgently as were German demands in Tokyo—and frequently with as little appreciation of the ally's own needs—Japanese demands were not primarily for raw materials, but for manufactured products, including capital goods, and for German production techniques, blueprints, designs, and samples. Little is known about Japanese imports from Germany through regular commercial channels during the first year of the war. Though there was some curtailment of deliveries, it is by no means impossible that some heavy German equipment reached Japan or Manchuria. Most of it would have come on orders placed before the war by private Japanese companies; the Japanese or Manchurian governments probably played only a small role, if any, in securing or contracting for any of these imports.

A Japanese government program for German aid to the Japanese economy was formulated only in the summer and fall of 1940 in the course of the negotiations and deliberations which preceded the Tripartite Pact. By this time it had proved impossible to negotiate a new economic treaty with the United States; furthermore, as America began to embargo a number of commodities which Japan needed for her war economy and which she had traditionally procured in the United States, the Japanese became increasingly dissatisfied with their economic dependence on that country. Closer ties with the one remaining industrial power which did not oppose her foreign policy became one of Japan's chief objectives during the summer and autumn of 1940.

The Japanese thought of German economic and technological aid both in immediate and in long-range terms. Short-term aid, they expected, would be forthcoming in the shape of German machine tools, armaments, and a few critical raw materials. In the long run, they expected German technical know-how to benefit their own synthetic industries, thus lessening Japanese dependence on foreign supplies of strategic raw materials. German investment goods, particularly heavy equipment needed in such processes as the production of synthetic rubber and oil, and German aid in the development of the Japanese armaments and airplane industries, seem to have been under consideration in Tokyo in the fall of 1940.

Other Japanese officials thought that it was not too early to secure promises of future German investment in Greater East Asia so as to prevent German postwar capital exports from going to the Soviet Union alone.[28] Some Japanese seem to have contemplated a fairly drastic reorientation of the Japanese industrial economy, so far largely patterned on and supplied by the American economy. As one foreign ministry official explained, in the jargon of another era which pitted the "have-not" against the "have" nations:

> America's heavy industry is rich in materials. In other words, it is a heavy industry of the rich—and Germany's is that of the poor. As for Japan, it is necessary for her to learn Germany's poor man's heavy industry.[29]

In pursuit of these goals, the Japanese secured a

general German promise of technical assistance in the first secret annex to the Tripartite Pact. Simultaneously, the Japanese cabinet formally decided on September 27, 1940, to seek technological aid from the new ally; shortly, the Japanese began to survey specific needs and to formulate a program to be submitted to Berlin. To collect further information and present Japanese demands, the Japanese army and navy each dispatched a mission to Berlin in December 1940. The missions were headed by General Tomoyuki Yamashita (later to be known as the "Tiger of Malaya"), who stayed in Berlin from January to June 1941, and Admiral Naokuni Nomura, who stayed on there until 1943 and became the Japanese member of the Tripartite military committee.[30]

Shortly after their arrival in Berlin, the Japanese missions in early February 1941 presented their demands to the German government. The itemized lists have not been found, but the demands seem to have been substantial in the fields of artillery, radar and optical equipment, submarine and airplane models and parts, precision instruments and machine tools.[31] Among the German services, only the navy's response to the Japanese requests is known. In view of the navy's close interest in strategic cooperation with Japan at this time, its reservations about the Japanese aid program are particularly interesting. The navy recommended that only those requests be granted which would enable Japan to take effective military action against the Anglo-American powers in the near future. Deliveries which would only strengthen Japan's war potential some years hence ought not to be made, and all Japanese attempts at industrial "espionage" should be forestalled.[32]

Similarly, German business was reluctant to turn

over to the Japanese secret manufacturing techniques which, it feared, Japan might divulge to the United States or exploit to Germany's disadvantage in the postwar market.[33] Luckily for the Japanese missions, the doubts of the navy and of business circles were not shared by OKW and Hitler. Whatever their concern about the economic consequences of armaments aid to Japan, Hitler and the OKW were convinced that the military advantages of such assistance were on Germany's side. They were convinced that Japan stood ready to strike at Britain in the Far East, and that assurance of German technical aid would embolden the Japanese to open hostilities. Whether the Japanese had intentionally fostered this illusion in Berlin to obtain deliveries or whether they merely failed to correct Germany's misconception is not clear.

The connection between arms aid and the German hope for military cooperation against Britain can be traced in a number of statements which link the visit of the Japanese missions with the Führer directive of early March concerning military collaboration with Japan. Reporting on the requests of Admiral Nomura for arms and technical aid, General Jodl informed Hitler on January 29, 1941:

> The proposals of Admiral Nomura have raised the question of the German attitude towards military cooperation with Japan. One could deduce from them that Japan desired the formulation of joint operational plans of the three powers and intended to approach Germany and Italy with demands for materiel.[34]

Two weeks later, Hitler similarly linked the two issues when he gave directions for the drafting of the directive on cooperation with Japan:

> It was Germany's aim to cause Japan to act decisively in the Far East at the earliest opportunity. . . . Japan would have to capture Singapore. . . . In return, Germany should allow the Japanese a generous look at German war and combat experiences, and should give her permission to copy modern weapons and implements. That the present Japanese government would change its course seemed unlikely to him.[35]

The Führer directive on cooperation with Japan, issued on March 5, 1941, ordered the services to fulfill Japan's demands generously and comprehensively and not to insist on reciprocal benefits. But despite the order from Hitler, the Japanese made little progress with their negotiations in Berlin. A host of German ministries and agencies managed to delay the Japanese program for reasons which had little military relevance.

GERMAN HESITATIONS

The foreign ministry insisted that negotiations with the Japanese be conducted through it. The ministry was just then dispatching the Wohlthat mission to Tokyo and was determined to use Japanese requests for technical aid as a bargaining point in the negotiations for the general economic treaties which Wohlthat was instructed to discuss in Japan. To be in a position where it could bargain most advantageously, the foreign ministry insisted that all Japanese demands for technical and armaments aid be consolidated in one list (the so-called *Wunschliste*) and that no orders be placed with individual German firms until the list had been approved by the German government.[36] The Japanese services complied with the ministry's instructions; yet negotiations still made little progress.

The delay had several causes. For one thing, the foreign ministry had to obtain the views and coordinate the decisions of a large number of agencies, both military and civilian, which claimed the right to be heard in the matter of deliveries to Japan. If Japanese specifications on the consolidated list were insufficient, time-consuming queries for clarification had to be dispatched to Tokyo. Whether the political estrangement of Germany and Japan in the spring of 1941—particularly the beginning of the Japanese-American negotiations in April 1941—had any influence on the treatment of Japanese demands is not known.

The original Japanese list had not been acted upon when the outbreak of the Russo-German war and the closing of the Siberian route changed some of the basic assumptions underlying the Japanese program. Certain items in the Japanese list would have to be dropped; for example, a large airplane factory which was to have been built in Manchukuo with heavy German equipment that could only be brought over the land route. Under the changed circumstances, the Japanese reapplied for single samples, designs, and manufacturing licenses for a large number of the items they had previously expected to import in quantity, planning to construct in Japan what they could no longer obtain from the Reich. At the same time, Foreign Minister Ribbentrop instructed the economic division of the foreign ministry to scale down the Japanese *Wunschliste* so that it might be fulfilled under existing limitations of transport, ability to pay, and German production capacity.

It took the German authorities from June to September 1941 to agree on a scaled-down Japanese list. The reasons for the delay were explained in a memorandum, submitted along with the revised list, by the director of the economic division of the foreign ministry to Ribbentrop. The memorandum also assessed the potential political-military returns for technical aid more realistically than the OKW had in the preceding spring:

> The purpose of compiling [the reduced list] was to keep the Japanese on our side [*bei der Stange halten*] and to destroy any doubts they may have had concerning our readiness to support them, as far as possible, in the build-up of their armament and armaments industry.
>
> My efforts in compiling this reduced list have met considerable resistance among the [German] internal agencies; the military authorities plead reasons of military secrecy of weapons and procedures; the Economics Ministry and the Four-Year-Plan object to the transfer of valuable German intellectual property to a competitor on credit and without sufficient *quid pro quo;* all agencies finally object on the grounds that German industrial capacity is fully employed for our own production and leaves no room for deliveries to Japan.[37]

Though they realized that Germany's raw-material imports and possibly Japan's political friendship were at stake, the Germans continued to move slowly. The revised list was not even submitted to Japan before Pearl Harbor. Once Japan had come into the war, the Germans dropped some of their reservations about disclosing to her the latest German weapons developments. Yet the two countries remained far apart. A scaled-down German list (of 62 items) was finally presented to Japan in February 1942, only to be followed by a Japanese counterdemand for 216 items in early July 1942.[38] When the Germans countered with still another offer in August, its size was shaped by German foreign exchange needs as much as by the military needs of Japan.[39]

The Japanese would probably have been happy to purchase a sample or two of each of the items on the latest German list. With the help of such samples, they would start production in Japan. German industry and OKW, however, were reluctant to turn over samples of the most modern German equipment, unless Japan also purchased the expensive manufacturing licenses and technical data that went with each product.[40] The Japanese, confident that they could start production without the German data, and reluctant to pay the high costs of the licenses, appealed the issue to Hitler. As usual, the Führer gave a more favorable decision than had lower German echelons. Japan was to be sold samples, even if she did not acquire the licenses.[41] On the basis of Hitler's decision, OKW now gave security clearance for the items on the German list and the Japanese began to work out conditions of payment and delivery with the individual German manufacturers.

THE DIMENSIONS OF GERMAN AID

To give a quantitative picture of German assistance to the Japanese is impossible. It is clear that German deliveries were drastically limited by the shipping problem, just as were shipments from the Far East to Europe. The chief means of transport, in the absence of Japanese vessels, were the German and Italian blockade-breakers which went to the Far East to pick up raw materials for Germany. There is evidence that some of these ships departed for the Far East without being fully loaded. Presumably, the delay in negotiating the Japanese requests in Berlin or in obtaining delivery from the German manufacturer explained this situation. Since the ships were German and Italian and not Japanese, it is understandable that they followed a shipping schedule determined by German rather than Japanese needs and departure times.

During the 1941–1942 shipping season, eight ships reached the Far East; they carried a total cargo of 32,500 tons. During the 1942–1943 season, another eight ships reached the Far East, with a total cargo of 24,447 tons. No tabulation of losses incurred en route to the Far East is available. Originally, seven ships were slated to leave for the Far East during the 1943–1944 season, but in view of the heavy losses of ships returning from Asia during the previous shipping season and the general hazards of blockade breaking at the time, it is unlikely that more than one or at most two ships left. Whether any arrived is not known.[42]

After the second half of 1943, a total of twenty submarines reached the Far East in order to take cargo back to Europe. As some of the boats carried out assignments in the Indian Ocean before going to Japan, they could not have carried a full load of cargo. Nor did any of the Japanese submarines used in blockade breaking succeed in making the return trip to Japan. The total number of boats being limited, their capacity small, and the imports desired by the Japanese difficult to crate and pack on a submarine, Japan must have derived little benefit from this phase of blockade breaking.

The maximum freight that reached Japan by sea

during the period 1941–1944 was therefore in the neighborhood of 60,000 tons, roughly two-thirds of the amount that reached Germany on the more numerous voyages from the Far East. How much Germany had sent to Japan over the Siberian route prior to its closing is not known, but the amount probably did not match what the Germans received, since the Japanese government's program was only presented in early 1941 and not acted upon for another fifteen months.

Because of the kind of commodities acquired by the Japanese, a description in terms of amounts would be less informative than similar information about the German imports. A full description by type, though it would mean more, cannot be given, since the German and Japanese data are incomplete. It is possible, however, to indicate the general areas in which Japanese purchases were strongest, to list some of the more important German products disclosed and sold to the Japanese, and to indicate in very general terms the value which these purchases seem to have had for the Japanese war economy.[43]

The Germans shared with Japan a number of manufacturing techniques useful to the Japanese war economy—such as a special Krupp process for making cartridge steel and methods for the construction of barrel linings and for electric welding in the construction of naval vessels. Among finished war implements, the Japanese requested and obtained several pieces of artillery—the 10.5-centimeter and the 12.8-centimeter antiaircraft guns, Germany's famous 8.8-centimeter antiaircraft and antitank guns, and a 7.5-centimeter antitank piece. Some lighter artillery, including two types of machine guns, was also acquired by the Japanese. In view of Japan's general inferiority to Germany in artillery, all these acquisitions had great potential value to Japan. The value of the 10.5-centimeter antiaircraft gun was enhanced when Germany made available to her ally the combination radar-optical range finder and director which went with this caliber and which the Japanese could not match in quality.

Though it is not known what use Japan made of them, articles from the German optical industry must have been of great value to her. The German records disclose that numerous Leica cameras were given to the Japanese for reconnaissance, especially air reconnaissance, though manufacturing licenses and blueprints seem not to have been divulged, at least not by Leitz. The Japanese acquired a bombsight (specifications unknown), which was probably better than their own, though not as good as American models. A German stereoscopic range finder was also of great potential value.

Germany shared with Japan some of her developments in the radar field and in anti-enemy radar devices. Copies of the Würzburg and Rotterdam sets were turned over to the Japanese as was a homing device (unidentified).

In 1944, a Tiger tank was sold to Japan. Whether it reached Japan is not known. In view of Japan's inferiority in armor, reproduction of the Tiger tank in Japan might have become significant in the event of an Allied landing and protracted fighting on the Japanese home islands.

Among items for the Japanese navy, the Germans turned over a gun stabilizer for surface ships. This should have been very beneficial to the Japanese, who, though generally competent in gun control, were outclassed in this respect by the Germans. For that reason, too, the Japanese may have benefited from a torpedo fire control unit for surface ships which should have enabled them to make better use of their already excellent torpedoes. Further, Germany made available a 750-ton submarine hull, which probably aided Japanese ship designers since the German model was more pressure-resistant than any Japanese design. Finally, the Japanese acquired the German navy's automatic E-switch, a control device for computing and adjusting fire against enemy aircraft. Its use would have remedied a pronounced Japanese weakness.

Equipment for the Japanese air force would seem to have been of less value. Japan acquired specimens of the fighter planes Me-109 and FW 120, which probably were better than her own comparable types, although the United States had learned halfway through the war to cope with these planes on the European theater. A pursuit plane, the Me-163, and the jet Me-263 were also given to Japan. However, like Germany herself, Japan did not obtain and produce the jet early enough in the war to enable its superiority to offset the enemy's greater numbers.

During the early war years, the Germans released to Japan only those items which had passed beyond the development stage. Japan was offered access to V-1 and V-2 data but refused the latter.[44] Whether she acquired data on the submarine *Schnorchel* is not known.

It is difficult to measure the benefit which Japan derived from the German samples she acquired and the occasional manufacturing data she procured. Reproduction of the German-made items in Japan seems to have presented greater difficulties than either Germany or Japan at first expected. Possibly this was because Japanese engineers were not skillful enough and German technicians were sent to Japan only in rare cases. Shortages in labor and raw materials may also account for Japan's failure to make better use of the German samples and data.

Two examples illustrate this point. In 1943 Germany had presented Japan with two submarines. These were to be examined and copied to enable Japan to wage a more effective warfare against enemy merchant shipping, presumably mainly in the Indian Ocean. Of the two boats one was lost en route to the Far East, the other one was gratefully received, and even acknowledged in a personal telegram from Hirohito. Production of the boat, however, was never begun in Japan.[45]

Another notable example of the failure of technological assistance is the case of the German jet plane Me-263, then the only military jet in the world. A specimen of the Me-263 was acquired by the Japanese in 1944. When the plane and the accompanying Messerschmitt technicians were lost en route from Singapore to Japan, the Japanese tried to construct the plane from the blueprints, which had been flown ahead. Numerous delays occurred and instead of having the plane in production by March 1945, as they expected, the Japanese only flight-tested the first craft in July. It crashed. The story is told best in the words of the director of Mitsubishi's aircraft production division:

> Investigation disclosed that the engine failure was due to fuel feed stoppage. This was explained as follows: Because of the need for hurrying the test, Yokosuka airfield was used. This was known to be too small for safety so a minimum of fuel was loaded. So small an amount was loaded that, with high acceleration and

> steep angle-of-climb soon after take-off, the fuel surface dropped below the outlet level and the flow of fuel failed. As a result of this finding the whole fuel system had to be redesigned. The drain part was relocated and enlarged and a jet pump was installed. Before the next prototype engine could be built, however, the Japanese surrender occurred.[46]

Perhaps the Japanese were more successful in copying German products of less revolutionary design. Their representatives in Berlin certainly continued right up to early 1945 to send samples and blueprints to Japan—either by submarine or eventually by military courier via Turkey and the Soviet Union. Since the Japanese did not have to pay for manufacturing licenses and data after March 1944, however, it may well be that their sustained interest in German manufacturing methods reflected what the Germans chose to call "industrial espionage" rather than the expectation of concrete military benefits.

If German technical aid was of limited value to the Japanese services and Japan's wartime industry, one explanation can certainly be found in the lateness of the aid. The attempt to make up for lost time played a fatal role in the crash of the test jet. Loss of time and delay of negotiations in Berlin also meant that the German designs reached Japan when she was no longer able to take full advantage of them. By 1944, when many of the most important German designs reached Japan, her industry was already too badly disrupted by her disastrous supply situation and the massive American air raids to permit her to put German-made items into serial production.

PRIVATE BENEFITS AND PUBLIC VICES

The delays may reflect certain inadequacies in Japanese planning procedures, as the German authorities complained from time to time. More often, they resulted from the inability of the Nazi regime to subordinate private or militarily irrelevant interests to the major objective of winning the war. Even after Hitler had promised generous support of the Japanese aid program in the spring of 1941, subordinate German government agencies invoked nonmilitary considerations, including pleas from industry to protect future profits, to delay or subvert a program which ought to have been of vital interest to the Nazi regime. The interplay between private and public interests can be illustrated by certain aspects of the German-Japanese negotiations about manufacturing licenses (*Nachbaurechte*).

When the revised list of items was cleared by Hitler in August 1942, Japan was free to enter into direct negotiations with the German manufacturers about samples and manufacturing licenses, technical data (*Erfahrungen*) and know-how. Although Hitler had ruled that Japan need not purchase a license for every sample she acquired, the Japanese apparently found it in their interest to acquire numerous licenses. Presumably only the sale of a manufacturing license would induce the German manufacturer to surrender the technical data and blueprints which would make production in Japan feasible at an early time.

As soon as the Japanese approached the German companies about the sale of manufacturing licenses, disagreements over prices arose. The Japanese complained that they were being overcharged and insisted that the German prices would soon exhaust the one billion yen (586 million Reichsmark) credit Japan had obtained in January 1943. The Japanese accusations seem to have been justified in a number of instances. In fact, there is evidence that the German government had instructed German patent-holders to increase their charges in order to compensate for the rubber prices in Asia which Germany thought had been artificially raised by the Japanese.[47]

By February 1943 some German authorities suggested that the Japanese submit the matter to Hitler for reconsideration and determination of a fair price. The Japanese, however, raised a more radical demand. They insisted that the profit motive should not enter the relations between allies at all and that Germany should turn her manufacturing licenses and designs over without compensation.[48] Among the German governmental agencies who dealt with the Japanese and among the interested German companies there was considerable opposition to this demand. The ministry of economics rejected the Japanese argument, and insisted on "sufficient export prices" (*"auskömmliche Exportpreise"*).[49] The military admitted that Japan was being charged many times what some of Germany's present enemies had paid for identical licenses before the war. They recommended that a new and fair price be decided upon by OKW.[50]

In May 1943 Hitler handed down the basic decision. As usual, it was more favorable to the Japanese point of view than had been the preliminary decisions of lower German echelons. Hitler decreed that wherever feasible Japan ought to be given manufacturing rights and relevant designs immediately. Terms of payment should be worked out as speedily as possible, but delivery should not be made dependent on a settlement of the financial question. Only "moderate export prices" were to be demanded, and in no case should disagreement over terms prevent the dispatch of the item in question by blockade-breaker.[51]

In the interpretation of the order, subordinate agencies reserved sufficient flexibility to insure that German economic interests would not be damaged by Hitler's generosity. OKW instructed the German firms that if time were needed to "complete the data" for delivery to the Japanese it might be exploited (*ausnutzen* is the term) to press German price demands on the Japanese. In addition, OKW insisted that the Führer's terms should apply only to those German manufactures which were "war implements" under German terms of classification. Whenever the copying of a war implement involved disclosure of techniques and procedures which were of more than strictly military relevance, the manufacturing rights should be granted and the data made available only *after* Japan had made satisfactory arrangements about payment.[52]

It is not surprising that the Japanese had further occasion to complain of overcharging and deliberate German delays. In June 1943 they renewed their request to obtain manufacturing licenses and data free of charge for the duration of the war. The German government took the matter under advisement. After much soul-searching by the lower echelons and several alternative proposals, Hitler decided in early 1944 to accede to the Japanese request. On March 2, an agreement was concluded between the two governments, under which both nations would put important war materials at each other's disposal without payment. The financial settlement would be determined "after the final victory" and in the meantime the German government undertook to compensate the German patent-holders for any licenses and techniques that Japan was given.[53]

It is instructive to compare the Axis settlement of this question with the solution of similar problems among their wartime opponents. The practice at which the Axis finally arrived in early 1944 seems to have been adopted between the United States and Britain as early as the fall of 1940. No royalties were charged to Packard by the British, who in the fall of 1940 permitted the American company to produce for the United States Air Corps the battle-proven Merlin engine, a product of Rolls Royce.[54] Whether the British government undertook to reimburse Rolls Royce or whether the British company waived all royalty rights in the interest of the war effort (a practice later adopted by some American companies in the synthetics field) is not known. In either case, the Allies had proved capable of subordinating private gain to the common national purpose much earlier than their opponents, even while Axis propaganda concentrated on the enemy's addiction to "plutocracy."

Under the Lend-Lease Act, a slightly different arrangement was adopted. Governments receiving lend-lease shipments from the United States agreed to reimburse any American citizen whose patent rights had been adversely affected by the transfer of a defense article or information under the lend-lease agreement.[55] Perhaps this comparison is not quite so apt, however, since lend-lease involved mainly the transfer of manufactured items or raw materials or services, rather than the disclosure of industrial processes and know-how.

In addition to the irritation and delay caused by

haggling over prices, the German government bound procedures in red tape by requiring the Japanese to purchase all equipment through the old German trading companies in East Asia, the *Ostasienhäuser.*[56] The Japanese, using an extensive staff in the attachés' offices in Berlin, would have preferred to purchase directly from the German manufacturers, many of whom had not been in the Far Eastern business before. To protect those firms which had been in the Asian market and perhaps to compensate them for the losses suffered earlier from Japanese commercial practices in China and Manchuria, the German Ministry of Economics decreed that unless a company had had a branch office in the Far East before the war it could not sell to the Japanese directly but would have to transact its business through one of the established firms. Although the requirement would not slow down negotiations in the same way that the financial disagreements did, it could not but add to the cumbersome and time-consuming procedure which had already hamstrung Germany's aid to Japan.

There was a third major difficulty in the transfer of manufacturing licenses, which even Hitler's decision of early 1944 did not solve. It concerned the protection of German patent-holders against Japanese competitors, should the information given to Japanese companies for wartime purposes be used after the war to infringe on German markets. Whether paid by the Japanese or compensated by the German government, the German patent-holders were determined to deny Japan any such advantage. The German companies therefore drew up elaborate clauses for insertion in the licensing contract, by which Japan promised not to use the German techniques except for production on government orders and during the war. This led to considerable unpleasantness between the German patent-holders and the Japanese services, who were the formal recipients of the licenses. The clauses, which seemed to the Germans a protection of their intellectual property, appeared to the Japanese as an insult to their honor.[57] The matter no doubt was complicated by the differences in German and Japanese patent law and the lack of a German-Japanese patent agreement.

Eventually the German government drafted at Japan's request a model license contract which all German patent-holders might follow. There is evidence that the contracts concluded between the Japanese services and individual German companies followed this government draft almost verbatim. By the fall of 1943 the guarantee it contained had become a standard feature of all German-Japanese licensing contracts.[58]

SYNTHETIC OIL: A CASE HISTORY

While German-Japanese negotiations about armaments and related equipment gave ample scope to private German interests, one episode, involving the German chemical industry, illustrates better than others the Nazi government's inability or unwillingness to subordinate private interest to her ally's need. This concerned the negotiations between the Japanese government and IG Farbenindustrie A. G. about the synthetic production of oil by the hydrogenation process.

Japan had first shown an interest in German techniques of synthetic oil production during the mid-1930s. In 1936 Mitsui had acquired a manufacturing license for the Fischer-Tropsch process from the German patent-holder, Ruhrchemie. This was meant to strengthen Japan's own as yet insignificant synthetic oil industry. After 1937 synthetic oil production, particularly in Manchuria, received strong backing from the Japanese government under a new plan for the development of Japan's natural and synthetic oil resources.[59] When the manufacturing techniques available in Japan were judged inadequate to fulfill the plan's goals, the Japanese government in the late 1930s approached IG Farben with a request for a manufacturing license for the hydrogenation process.

The delicacy of the subsequent negotiations was largely due to the peculiar status of the hydrogenation patent. The inventor of the process, Dr. Friedrich Bergius, had sold his patent to IG Farben in the mid-1920s and that company, in turn, had sold it to the Standard Oil Company (New Jersey) in 1927. After this date, IG Farben merely retained hydrogenation rights for Germany, and a 20-per-cent royalty in the rights and processes sold to Standard Oil. In 1931, Standard Oil turned its foreign (non-U.S.) hydrogenation patent rights over to its subsidiary, International Hydrogenation Patents Company (IHP) in The Hague. A half-interest in that company was later sold to Royal Dutch–Shell.[60] IG Farben's sale of the patent rights outside Germany also limited the dispositions which the company could make in regard to its technical data (*Erfahrungen*) in the hydrogenation field. Potentially the most valuable of IG Farben's possessions in the eyes of the Japanese, the technical data could only be sold to a properly licensed party, at least according to IG's agreement with Standard Oil.[61]

When the Japanese army in 1938 attempted to acquire a manufacturing license for hydrogenation, it should have gone to IHP which held the licensing rights for the Far East. Considering IHP too closely allied with British and American oil interests, the Japanese instead turned to IG Farben. The German company, evidently pleased at Japan's new interest in the hydrogenation technique, transmitted the Japanese request to IHP. IG Farben probably expected or knew that the Japanese army, as soon as it had obtained the license, would turn to IG for technical data and the use of IG engineers in the establishment of the first hydrogenation units in Japan.

By December 1938, IHP had notified IG Farben that Japan could be given a license, provided IG remitted 80 per cent of the royalties to IHP. The matter rested here for some time, because IG Farben in early 1939 had begun to lose interest in the Japanese project. It turned out that the Japanese plan was merely to build a plant to produce 15,000 tons of oil per year; IG Farben was apparently reluctant to part with its technical data for the sake of so small a contract. Later in the year, however, IG Farben's views once more changed. The company discovered that the Japanese planned to use hydrogenation of tars rather than of coal. Under these circumstances, IG Farben was ready to sell Japan its data on tar hydrogenation while retaining its more valuable data on the hydrogenation of coal.

On this basis, a preliminary contract (*Vorvertrag*) was concluded between IG Farben and Mitsubishi, acting for the Japanese army, in the fall of 1939. A Japanese army mission was expected in Germany at the end of the year to settle final details. Before the negotiations had proceeded to this stage, however, highly political considerations were introduced by a third party, the American government, which brought Japanese efforts to a temporary halt.

In its attempt to exert mild but steady economic pressure on Japan, the American government in late 1939 insisted that no American company holding patent rights for synthetic oil production should license a Japanese manufacturer. The government's moral embargo extended to foreign companies in which American firms had a controlling interest. On instructions from its American parent company, Standard Oil, IHP in December 1939 informed IG Farben that the preliminary contract with Mitsubishi had to be canceled.

If the American government invoked political motives to disrupt the German-Japanese business negotiations, IG Farben's own commercial interests dictated that the company fall in line with the American decision. The Japanese contract was not lucrative enough to warrant the application of pressure on IHP or the breach of a contract. From the company's point of view, this was not the time to strain relations with IHP or its American parent company, particularly since an IHP hydrogenation license for the Soviet Union was needed before IG Farben could proceed with a large and profitable hydrogenation project there. The IG records suggest that it was mainly the scale of the Russian project which caused the company to favor the Soviet Union over Japan; there is no evidence that the German government had influenced this choice for political reasons. From December 1939 to August 1940 the Japanese project made no progress. Most likely the Japanese did not press very hard after they had been turned down in December. They renewed their request for a hydrogenation license, however, after the American government had embargoed the export of aviation gasoline to Japan in late July. The Japanese now contemplated much bigger facilities than before; they spoke of a plant producing 100,000 tons of oil per year. The more ambitious dimensions of the Japanese project rekindled the interest of some IG Farben representatives. Since the Russian project had meanwhile been abandoned, consideration of that, it was thought, need no longer influence IG's stand on the Japanese request. Some company spokesmen advocated the sale of IG's technical data to Japan regardless of the solution of the complicated licensing question. Recommending this course of action to the company's directors, IG's Büro Sparte I thought that the German government might be prevailed upon to order IG Farben to go through with the sale of its technical data—a not unreasonable expectation at a time when Germany and Japan were drawing together politically, and the United States had begun to support Britain. Should the company act under government orders, the Büro concluded, Standard Oil would surely "understand" the political necessity which was forcing IG Farben to break its contract.[62]

The advocates of this view were soon overruled by higher echelons in the company. By early September 1940 IG Farben officially declared that the fulfillment of Japanese wishes in contravention of the company's contractual obligations to Standard Oil was opposed to the best interest of the company. Profits from the Japanese project were judged insufficiently attractive to warrant the very considerable risk of reprisals at the hands of Standard Oil to which IG Farben might expose itself. Since the company recognized the political implications of the Japanese request, however, it was willing to leave the final decision up to the German government.

By November 1940 the government had decided not to overrule the company's arguments. Whether the government thought that political considerations were irrelevant or held that Germany's political interest coincided with the interests of the company is not certain. At any rate neither the company nor the government changed its mind when Japan pursued the matter through her embassy in Berlin.

The basic reasons underlying IG Farben's stand are set forth with great candor in the company records over the next few months. One consideration which weighed heavily with the company was the fear of reprisals should IG Farben give its data to the Japanese in the face of IHP's ban on the license. The company thought it likely that in case of a contract violation Standard Oil might well sue in the courts of neutral countries in which IG Farben had extensive assets. The American company was thought to stand a good chance of being awarded damages out of IG Farben assets.

Throughout much of 1941 the company also seems to have suspected the Japanese of pursuing the license and data question as a mere blind to cover their quest for IG Farben technicians and German hydrogenation equipment. These, the company feared, would be used to improve Japan's own hydrogenation technique. The company was therefore determined not to part with its specialists or its costly technical data unless the Japanese also purchased the license and the data. IHP's refusal to sanction the license relieved IG Farben of the need to disclose its true objections to the Japanese.

But fear of reprisals alone did not determine IG's

policy. The company did not wish to damage its close and profitable relations with Standard Oil, particularly the patent exchanges in the synthetics field which the two companies had entered into in 1930. Though exchanges of data had been broken off shortly after the outbreak of the war in Europe, IG Farben considered the suspension temporary and was ready to subordinate most other matters, including the Japanese project, to the preservation of amicable working relations with Standard Oil after the war.[63] While this consideration may have weighed most heavily with the company, in its communications to the German government IG naturally stressed the loss of foreign exchange should the company assets in neutral countries be forfeited as a result of court action.

The argument about loss of foreign assets may have counted heavily with the Nazi government. Whether it is the only explanation for the government's refusal to aid its Japanese ally is not known. During his visit to Berlin in the spring of 1941 Foreign Minister Matsuoka discussed the hydrogenation project with IG Farben representatives in the presence of government officials. IG referred on this occasion to the "contractual difficulties" which stood in the way of the Japanese project, and Matsuoka pointed out in conclusion that if the procurement of oil through synthetic production proved impossible, Japan would simply have to go and "get her oil."[64] It is possible that the German government thought it could encourage Japanese expansion in Southeast Asia by withholding German aid in the hydrogenation field. Such an explanation is consistent with German policy during the spring of 1941, although no evidence for such a Machiavellian scheme has been found.

The scant evidence for the second half of 1941

rather points in another direction. Economic, not political, considerations still dominated the German government in the hydrogenation question as late as October 1941. By then, Foreign Minister Ribbentrop had approved the Japanese request for licenses and data, primarily at the insistence of the Wohlthat delegation and the German embassy in Tokyo; it was the ministry of economics that still held out against the Japanese, and although its precise grounds are not known, they were most probably of an economic nature. The ministry's assent had apparently not yet been secured when Pearl Harbor and the German declaration of war against the United States changed the picture. Ribbentrop ordered IG Farben to accede to the Japanese request for technical data. A consideration of IG's relations with the American company, he insisted in early 1942, was no longer appropriate.

Faced with this demand, IG Farben sought to comply in a manner best calculated to safeguard its own and Standard Oil's financial interests in the hydrogenation patent. Theoretically, at least two ways of circumventing the still existing legal obstacles against giving Japan the data suggested themselves to IG Farben. One method was based on the happy circumstance that a branch of IHP had remained in Holland when the company itself had moved to the western hemisphere shortly before the German invasion of the Netherlands. If Germany chose to consider the branch of IHP in The Hague as the patent-holder and applied pressure on the hapless Dutch, a hydrogenation license for the Japanese would no doubt be forthcoming, either directly from IHP or, with IHP's assent, through IG Farben. The other method would have had Japan declare that she had acquired the hydrogenation license by compulsory licensing. In either case, IG Farben would be free to negotiate with the Japanese about the sale of its technical data, by then the true object of all Japanese efforts. If the first method was chosen, the Japanese would have to pay whatever price the Germans, in conjunction with IHP, put on the license. In this case, IG Farben was ready to put the royalties in a special account for later settlement with IHP and Standard Oil after the war. The second method would enable the Japanese to acquire the license for a nominal fee or at no expense at all. After some wavering, IG decided to pursue the first course.[65]

In early June 1942 representatives of the Dutch IHP and IG Farben worked out an arrangement whereby IHP granted IG Farben a *Generallizenz* which would entitle IG, in turn, to license the Japanese and sell them its own techniques. The financial terms contemplated by the Germans and the Dutch at this stage of the negotiations are not known. At any rate, before the German-Dutch agreement had been in effect very long, IG Farben began to express doubt that the Japanese would recognize IG's *Generallizenz.* If Japan discovered that the license was of such recent date and had been acquired from an enemy alien, she would no doubt refuse to cooperate with IG Farben's plan.

The Japanese fell out of step, but for different reasons. IG Farben, proceeding on the course chosen, by early July 1942 had drafted a licensing agreement with the Japanese army on the basis of the *Generallizenz;* the draft was submitted to the foreign ministry and the ministry of economics for approval. From the available IG Farben records it would seem that the matter was then stalled for the next three months. If this was indeed the case, one reason may perhaps be found in Japan herself. Now that the Japanese had conquered the oil resources of the Dutch East Indies and were bringing them back into production, the pressure on Berlin for a hydrogenation license may well have relaxed. There is at least indirect evidence for this conjecture in the fact that the Japanese government during 1942 sharply reduced the priority of its own domestic oil industry, both synthetic and natural, in unrealistic reliance on the continued availability of southern oil supplies.[66] But by October 1942 the Japanese resumed their negotiations with IG Farben. During 1943, as American submarines took an ever-growing toll of Japanese tankers bringing oil from the south, the urgency of their requests must have mounted.

Still the Germans would not be rushed. Between October 1942 and August 1943, the negotiations were deadlocked over the legal issue of Japan's license. As IG Farben had feared, the Japanese government contended that it need not purchase a license at all, since it had already acquired all of IHP's patent rights in the Far East by compulsory licensing. Hence, the Japanese argued, the sole object of their future negotiations was IG Farben's technical data, for which Japan was prepared to pay "adequate compensation." The Japanese also declared that they were ready to acquire a license for any IG hydrogenation patents taken out after Pearl Harbor day, since the compulsory license was held to cover only rights existing prior to that day. During the spring and early summer of 1943, IG Farben refused to accept the Japanese version of the legal issues at stake. The real reasons for the company's position are not entirely clear: perhaps it really felt bound by its recent licensing contract with IHP; perhaps it refused to recognize compulsory licensing because of the financial loss to itself and IHP. Only pressure from the German government, the company argued, would force it to change its stand.[67]

The government was slow in applying such pressure. It may finally have done so. At any rate, in August 1943, IG Farben declared itself ready to recognize the compulsory license acquired by Japan and to proceed with negotiations about technical data and post-Pearl Harbor patents.[68]

Despite the agreement on the legal issues, negotiations about the technical data continued for another eighteen months. The IG Farben records suggest at least two reasons for the further delay: IG's continued uneasiness over the recognition of Japan's compulsory license, and disagreement over the financial terms of a settlement. IG's qualms over the legal situation are sufficiently evident from the company's insistence on a written assurance from the German government that the sale of the data had taken place at the government's behest. Without such a declaration, the company was unwilling to conclude its contract with the Japanese.[69]

In addition, disagreements over the price and payment schedule for IG Farben's technical data delayed the conclusion of the agreement. The company's records for 1944 are sparse but there is evidence that the financial terms of the final settlement were not entirely satisfactory to the company. It can only be surmised, therefore, that IG Farben held out against such terms as long as it could. Whether the German government eventually prevailed on the company to settle on Japan's terms is not known.

It was not until January 11, 1945, that the Japanese

military attaché, General Komatsu, and representatives of the company concluded the final contract. IG Farben agreed to sell the Japanese war minister a license on all IG's hydrogenation rights and, more important, all the company's data and processes, on the further understanding that Japan had already acquired IHP's hydrogenation rights by compulsory licensing. The price for IG's rights and data was fixed at 18 million Reichsmark, which included payment for technical assistance, which IG promised to furnish in the establishment of the first three hydrogenation units in Japan. Of this sum, 20 per cent was payable upon conclusion of the agreement, 30 per cent within six weeks after the transfer of the data, and the remaining 50 per cent in five installments over a five-year period.[70]

The remainder of the hydrogenation story is fragmentary. In the IG Farben records there is evidence that the first installment was paid on February 16, almost five weeks after the agreement was signed, and one week after certain data (*Zeichnungen und Bestellentwürfe*) had been turned over to the Japanese. Whether a complete set of the data was ever delivered to the Japanese is not known. Nor is it clear how much IG Farben was paid in the remaining few weeks of the war.[71]

There can be little doubt that the transfer of data, if it did indeed take place, came far too late to do Japan any good. The German government certainly bears some responsibility for the interminable delays in the negotiations; it alone could have overruled the legitimate but militarily irrelevant considerations which had prevented IG Farben from sharing its knowledge with the Japanese at a time when such assistance might still have benefited the German-Japanese cause.

THE AXIS POWERS AT BAY

5

George Kennan has reminded us that the Second World War "was prejudiced, as a military encounter, before it was begun."[1] With the larger share of the world's land forces under the control of one or another totalitarian power (Germany, Japan, Russia), Kennan argues, only Japan could conceivably be defeated by the Western democracies alone, unaided by one of the other totalitarian powers. To defeat Germany and Russia combined was beyond the strength of the democracies; to defeat either one (or either one allied with Japan) would require the military aid of the other and hence prejudice any emerging peace settlement.

A similar logic of force, dictated by the same balance of power, governed the Axis alliance. Cooperating closely, Germany and Japan might have bested *either* the Western powers *or* the Soviet Union; taking on both adversaries at the same time proved fatal. The Japanese grasped the logic of power more clearly than the Germans and refused throughout the Second World War to attack Russia or provoke the Soviets into hostility. The foolhardiness of their German ally in attacking both Russia and the Western powers at the same time induced that "strange alliance" which in the end worked as much to Japan's as to Germany's detriment.

If political prudence and military necessity combined to bring the Western powers and Russia together after June 1941, common sense should have suggested to the Tripartite powers in 1940 and early 1941 that they coordinate policies and not endanger the alliance as a whole by the uncoordinated and unilateral acts of any member. Good sense the Axis powers lacked; hence they wasted the advantage which geographic position might have given them in a war against either the Western powers or the Soviet Union. The famous Axis "vise," which was meant to crush the opponent by simultaneous attacks from east and west, was simply unhinged as soon as Britain, the Soviet Union, and America had come together. Henceforth the Axis would be crushed in a superior vise, applied first to Germany, later to Japan.

The Tripartite Pact had rapidly lost focus during 1941 as first Germany, then Japan, by unilateral acts challenged and brought into the war their two most powerful adversaries. Still, the Axis's head start in armaments and the initial victories they gained through their surprise attacks in June and December 1941 left them considerable elbowroom in early 1942. During that year, however, failing to take a joint strategic initiative, they frittered away their limited assets in further uncoordinated ventures. By the autumn of 1942 they had gravely vitiated their power to win the war. But neither the German nor the Japanese government would then admit as much, either to its ally or to itself.

The areas for potential German-Japanese cooperation were seriously reduced by early 1943: militarily, they might join forces in an attack on the global Allied supply system that was surely one of the key elements in the Allied recovery of initiative throughout 1943; diplomatically, the Tripartite powers might cooperate to fracture the enemy coalition. The dismal failure of the Germans and Japanese to press a coordinated attack against enemy shipping illustrates the difficulties they faced in implementing joint plans, even when a rare consensus on objectives had been reached.

THE WAR ON ENEMY SHIPPING

The Japanese navy had initially prepared for the

classic battles of fleet against fleet (including air arms on both sides). Japan tended to assign a lowly place to warfare against enemy shipping, and her sinkings of enemy tonnage proved very disappointing to the German navy, accustomed as it was, especially after Germany's loss of her battle fleet, to give primacy to the war against enemy supply lines. Japan sank less shipping in the whole of 1942 than German submarines had during the first four months of the year. Even more grievous from the German point of view, Japan in 1942 hardly managed to make a dent in the Allied supplies flowing through the western Indian Ocean into both the Soviet Union and North Africa.[2]

Upon repeated German urging, the Japanese appeared ready in early 1943 to revise their ideas about the role of the war against merchant shipping in the total Axis effort. But it was not easy to translate resolve into action. Her submarine crews, used to operating as part of the surface fleet, required training in new methods of fighting. She was short in the types of boats most needed for the war on merchant ships and requested German help. Hitler was ready to extend it, though the navy was skeptical about its being used efficiently. In early 1943 Germany turned over to Japan two submarines which were to serve as models for serial production in Japan.[3] If the change of heart on Japan's part was gratifying to the German navy, the results of the submarine transfer proved as disappointing as the navy had foreseen. The boats left for the Far East only after a delay. One of them was lost in transit; the other was graciously received, but serial production was not begun, either because of a shortage of materials or of labor, or for some other reason. In the event, Japan sank even less shipping in 1943 than 1942.[4]

To increase the toll of enemy ships, Japan in late 1942 had also invited German submarines into the Indian Ocean, where they had not previously operated. The Japanese promised to make bases available, working out the necessary arrangements by the spring of 1943. From the summer of 1943 on, a number of German submarines operated out of Southeast Asian ports. They sank about one million GRT (Gross Register Tons) during the remainder of the war.[5]

The Japanese invitation probably reflected Japan's particular fears in the winter of 1942–1943. With the Allied victories in North Africa arose a danger that the Mediterranean would once more be opened to Allied shipping and that Britain's supply line to India would be considerably shortened. The first British convoy through the Mediterranean since mid-1940 took place in May 1943, shortly before German boats began to operate from Japanese bases in the Indian Ocean.

Yet all these German-Japanese efforts at joint submarine warfare came at least a year too late. By the spring of 1943 Allied radar began to cause a frightful toll among Axis submarines, and Allied replacements for the first time in over two years began consistently to outstrip German sinkings. The attack against merchant shipping could no longer "decide" the war, as the German navy had so recently argued in its attempts to invigorate this phase of Japanese warfare.

THE GREAT CONTRADICTION: RUSSIA

With the submarine weapon blunted, there remained the possibility of diplomatic action to retrieve some of the military disasters and to impart to the alliance that unity of purpose which it had not before enjoyed. The Japanese, not at war with the

Soviet Union, favored a separate German-Soviet peace. But after their earlier proposals along this line, in October 1941 and March 1942, had been turned down, they were reluctant to press the matter officially. During the spring of 1943 their advice to Berlin was contradictory—the Japanese navy offered its mediation for a separate peace with Russia, preferably after some German victories in the summer offensive; Japan's diplomats suggested that the Germans refrain from another round of costly summer battles.[6] While the Japanese foreign minister did not officially propose Japanese mediation, he was clearly interested in the efforts reportedly made by Bulgaria toward that end, and Japanese diplomats in Italy agreed with Italian leaders on the need to stop the Axis blood-letting in the east.[7] Germany chose not to involve Japan when during the summer of 1943 she put out feelers to Soviet representatives in Sweden to discover the terms of a possible peace.[8] Nothing was to come of these efforts in any case, if only because Hitler was never able to make up his mind. The German summer offensive was short-lived, and the victories which Hitler claimed he needed as a base for negotiations eluded him. Simultaneously, the Soviets and the Western powers composed some of the differences which had nourished the rumors—and perhaps in Japan the hopes—of a Soviet deal with Hitler; Soviet forces meanwhile enjoyed victories which made Moscow even less inclined to a separate peace.

By the fall of 1943 the military balance had tipped too far against the Germans to give hope of a separate German-Russian agreement. The suggestion of the Japanese foreign minister in January 1944 that Germany negotiate with Russia came to nothing.[9]

When the Japanese tried again late that summer, they met disbelief in Berlin that Stalin would be ready to negotiate. Indeed, the Soviet Union refused to receive the emissary whom Japan meant to send to Moscow for mediation.[10] Japan's belated attempt to reorient the war by diplomacy and to salvage most of the shrinking Axis force for action against *her* opponents had failed.

There is some doubt whether a German-Russian peace could ever have produced the results the Japanese expected. Even if it had been worked out in 1943, it would hardly have freed many German troops for action against the Western powers. Hitler was probably right when he explained in December 1942 that even if a new "Brest-Litovsk" line might be found (which he doubted), a separate peace would be only a truce and would still require him to keep substantial forces in the east.[11] Nor would Japan's other favored goal, the reopening of land communications with Germany, have brought the boon she expected in terms of a massive exchange of technical aid.

While the Japanese favored a German-Soviet peace, Berlin made fitful attempts to embroil the Japanese with the Soviet Union. It is hard to say which policy made worse sense as a means toward a common Axis victory. The Japanese policy was more realistic in that it recognized the limits of Tripartite capacities and the need for unity of purpose; its practical execution, however, was well-nigh impossible, given the military reality of Germany's eastern front and the political ambitions of the two contestants. A Japanese attack on Russia was, comparatively, a military possibility. Kwantung army and Red army forces in East Asia were about evenly matched through

1942.[12] And while Soviet forces may have been numerically larger from 1943 on, they were hardly the Soviet's best troops. Yet such an attack made no sense in the long run, politically or militarily. It would have dispersed the already overextended forces of the Tripartite powers and would have weakened Japan's defenses against the American counteroffensives. There was reasonable doubt whether a Japanese attack on Siberia would have relieved Germany sufficiently to warrant the additional burden on Japan, including attacks from the Maritime Provinces against the Japanese homeland.

Indeed, most German military leaders were fully aware of these arguments and many had consistently opposed Japan's entry into the war against Russia. Ribbentrop's earliest effort, in late June 1941, to induce the Japanese to attack Siberia probably even lacked Hitler's sanction.[13] After it had been rejected in early July 1941, the foreign minister, through the ambassador in Tokyo, still pursued this goal during the fall, even while the German navy counseled against the long-term commitment of Japanese forces in Siberia. Throughout 1942, neither Hitler, the navy, nor the army favored Japan's attack on the Soviet Union and Ribbentrop accordingly toned down his requests in Tokyo. Still, the foreign ministry insisted that Japan should enter the war against Russia *if her strength permitted.* In July 1942 Ribbentrop made such a strong plea for a Japanese attack on Russia that the Japanese once more held a liaison conference in which Berlin's suggestion was turned down in the most authoritative manner.[14] Ribbentrop's entreaties once more subsided, only to be again renewed after the defeat at Stalingrad. Once more the Japanese refused.[15]

Since OKH maintained at least until July 1943 that a Japanese attack on Siberia was on balance undesirable, the question arises as to whether Ribbentrop's requests to the Japanese in 1943, as in 1941, were undertaken on his own initiative. If he had the Führer's support, the whole episode is one more proof of the relegation of professional military judgment to second place.

The Japanese government seems not to have seriously contemplated a Siberian offensive after the summer of 1941. It promised to keep defenses in the north strong to tie down Soviet troops in Siberia and may in this manner have made a greater contribution to early German victories in Russia than it has usually been given credit for.[16] Only in 1943 and 1944 was the Kwantung army drastically reduced. On the other hand, Japanese protests against lend-lease and her occasional harassments of individual Soviet ships were on the whole ineffectual. They did not prevent the Pacific route from becoming the single most important channel for lend-lease deliveries to the Soviet Union.[17] German complaints on this score, especially in the later war years, are legion.

LAST DAYS AND RETROSPECT

By 1944 the Axis alliance had been reduced to a purely formal, lifeless arrangement, observed at appropriate dates by the exchange of congratulatory telegrams between Berlin and Tokyo. With Italy's removal from the war in 1943, even the formal unity of the Tripartite Pact had been broken. As Germany and Japan separately prepared to ward off Allied attacks on their interior defense lines, the opportunity for joint action between them all but disappeared. The Allied landing in France in June and the capture of Saipan (Marianas) in July 1944 breached the inner defenses of both Axis empires. Military disasters and their domestic repercussions—the attempt on Hitler's life and Tojo's resignation—had brought the Axis powers to bay by mid-1944. The following spring, Germany, too, broke the "no separate peace" pact by surrendering on May 8, without prior consultation with her ally. Himmler's and some generals' earlier attempts to surrender to the Western Allies only, while continuing the fight against Russia, struck the Japanese as perfidy. The Japanese foreign minister charged breach of treaty; the press noted a lack of *Bushido* in Germany and indulged in comparisons with the Badoglio regime. In what must have been one of its last diplomatic instructions, the German government blamed technical difficulties for its failure to consult the Japanese ally, denied any breach of commitment, and left it to Japan to renounce the treaties and break relations.[18] Thus the alliance ended—not with a bang but a whimper of mutual recrimination. Soon the victorious Allies proclaimed the call for Japan's surrender from the capital of her erstwhile ally.

The hollowness of the Axis alliance should have been apparent long before, had not the wartime mood induced both Axis and Allies to imagine a more united partnership than existed. Only since the end of the war has it been possible to discern the serious flaws in the Axis pact and to relate them to its final defeat.

One of the factors contributing to the defeat of the Axis was the disproportion between its own and its enemies' economic resources and capacity for industrial mobilization. Only the West's failure to take the Axis threat sufficiently seriously in the late 1930s permitted Germany and Japan to gain a temporary head start for war. Once the Western powers had grasped the extent of the danger and embarked on total mobilization of their resources, the Axis advantage was wiped out. In fact, from 1940 to 1942, Axis efforts at economic mobilization lagged behind the objective requirements of a "total war."[19] Only the defeats of 1943 induced the German and Japanese governments to embark on truly total mobilization of their industrial resources. In the light of the larger failure to grasp the requirements of war accurately, the failure of Germany and Japan to collaborate *as allies* in the economic and technological fields does not loom large. A more generous and expeditious exchange of raw materials and industrial products and data could have strengthened the war economies of both countries markedly, but only if the land route for bulk shipments had been kept open beyond mid-1941 and if a more stringent mobilization of all resources had been adopted by both governments at a much earlier date. Their failure to exploit the opportunity for economic assistance more fully thus points to the larger strategic contradiction that beset the alliance (and closed the land route between the two countries) and to their larger miscalculation about the economic requirements of total war.

One of the proverbial stumbling blocks in the path of any effective alliance is a serious disagreement over territorial matters. This factor played a subordinate role in the strains of the Axis alliance. On matters territorial, the Axis powers usually subordinated their individual territorial desires to a common concern: winning the war first. When ultimate territorial ambitions threatened to conflict with immediate military needs, the former were usually sacrificed.

Yet, upon closer inspection, the choice reflects not so much moderation and prudence as the essential absurdity of Axis territorial ambitions. Had either power approached the provisional dividing line, the 70th degree longitude, the incompatibility of their long-range territorial aims, particularly on Soviet territory, might well have been discovered. The discovery would then have corroded the last remnants of Axis solidarity. As it was, the military conquests of both Germany and Japan always fell far short of the spheres they had already assigned to each other and magnanimity was an easy virtue.

It was in the area of diplomatic and military coordination—in grand strategy and coalition warfare—that the German-Japanese alliance showed its greatest flaws from the outset. It is a moot question whether the failure was the more grievous in diplomatic or in military cooperation. Both trace back to the same intellectual deficiency, and together they reveal the inadequate conception of global conflict and of coalition warfare entertained by the two powers.

Some observers have maintained that the inadequacy of Axis military coordination, especially in 1942, was the fatal flaw in their effort. General George Marshall, for one, explained in 1948 that more effective Axis military coordination might well have delivered Eurasia into Axis hands by late 1942. He believed that "had the USSR and the British Army of the Nile been defeated in 1942, as they well might if the Germans, Japanese and Italians had better coordinated their plans and resources and successive operations, we should have stood today in the western hemisphere confronted by enemies who controlled a greater part of the world."[20]

It is true that Allied positions would have suffered grievously had Germany and Japan carried their offensives into the Indian Ocean in 1942. But it is important to remember that Germany had insufficient reserves to push her offensive very deeply into Egypt in the summer of 1942, particularly as long as the supply line across the Mediterranean continued to be insecure. The conquest of Egypt was thus not a simple possibility. In view of Japan's ability after March 1942 to expand beyond the original defense perimeter, one might argue that she at least had sufficient resources to embark on an attack on Ceylon and the British position in the Indian Ocean. Even assuming a Japanese capture of Ceylon, it is unlikely that a junction with German forces could have been brought about, or that it could have been maintained for any length of time. The Americans were convinced that in the last resort the Middle East must be held, and they would surely have come to the aid of the British in the Indian Ocean and North Africa if Axis efforts in the theater had been more energetic.

The more basic question in early 1942 was whether the Axis powers were still able to reorient their war effort so drastically that military cooperation in selected theaters would become feasible. Essentially this involved the question of their attitude toward the Soviet Union. Had Germany's and Japan's policies toward Russia been brought into line in 1942 (either by a Russo-German peace or by a Japanese attack on the Soviet Union), the Soviet recovery of strength in 1943 might have been prevented. Even so, Russia would have remained a strategic factor. A Russo-German truce would have tied down many German forces along an eastern European line. A joint German-Japanese invasion, even if successful, would have required large occupation forces on Russian soil. In the end, neither move might have freed enough Axis troops early enough to assure success of their joint venture in the Indian Ocean.

Even if either of these moves had made sense militarily, neither could be easily reconciled with long-established policies of the German and Japanese leadership. Hitler had long resolved to expand eastward; the Japanese, on the other hand, seem to have given up any serious thought of war against Russia after their unsuccessful battles along the border in the summer of 1939. Neither a Russo-German truce nor a Japanese attack on Siberia was thus a simple possibility. It would be more accurate to say that the Axis military partnership, dating from January 1942, never recovered the focus which the Axis political alliance had lost in 1941 when Germany's and Japan's separate and uncoordinated actions drove Russia and America into that "strange alliance" for which the Axis was no match.

Despite the diplomatic and military disarray that had come to mark the Axis pact after 1941, Germany and Japan reaped some of the advantages of strategic coordination without actually coordinating strategies. Their attacks forced Britain and America to wage war simultaneously in the Atlantic and Pacific; the profusion of military theaters and the interminable squabbles over priorities ("Europe first" versus "Asia first") strained the resources as well as the patience of Allied statesmen. At most, then, the coincidence in time of Axis moves forced the enemy to disperse their resources temporarily. But a temporary dispersal alone could not overcome the superior reserves of the enemy coalition. While the Axis powers reaped some of the advantages of geography—advantages they had inflated into a rather mechanical conception of geopolitical compatibility—they never seriously began to exploit the opportunities of their alliance.

Alliances between states are surely among the most fragile of political associations. The German-Japanese alliance was a failure, not only because each power failed separately to attain the goals it had set itself, but because as allies the powers failed to take advantage of their association. The failure resulted to a large extent from the discordance of their political goals and of the means necessary to attain them. To cite again merely the most obvious instances, Japan's conception of victory in the Greater East Asia war did not require the defeat of the Soviet Union, while Hitler's conception of a "new Europe" did. Similarly, Japan's realization of Greater East Asia, the Japanese thought, required a war with the United States, while Hitler's achievement of a "new Europe" initially did not.

Beyond this discordance and the Axis's unwillingness to face the fact of their diverging ambitions, the structures and ideologies of the two governments at the time made it difficult to achieve effective cooperation. The give-and-take that is required between sovereign nations for successful coalition warfare is difficult to obtain even under the most favorable circumstances: when nations are culturally akin; when their governments are accustomed to account to other men for their behavior; when rational analysis of ends and means prevails; and when the personalities of the leading statesmen prove congenial. Nobody would maintain that Germans and Japanese spoke the same language, despite the superficial similarity of their expansionist ideologies. While the Japanese military had established among themselves a tradition of consultation, deliberation, and compromise, they hardly felt accountable to their own civilian cabinet. The more rational component was likely to fade in the presence of a forceful or irrational man or group of men. In Germany, Hitler's personality and the *Führerprinzip* left no room for the process of rational analysis, consultation, and compromise from which alone joint decisions could emerge.

Appendix 1

The Tripartite Pact and Related Documents[1]

September 27, 1940.

A. Three Powers Pact between Germany, Italy and Japan

The Governments of Germany, Italy and Japan, considering it as the condition precedent of any lasting peace that all nations of the world be given each its proper place, have decided to stand by and co-operate with one another in regard to their efforts in Greater East Asia and the regions of Europe respectively wherein it is their prime purpose to establish and maintain a new order of things calculated to promote mutual prosperity and welfare of the peoples concerned.

Furthermore it is the desire of the three Governments to extend co-operation to such nations in other spheres of the world as may be inclined to put forth endeavours along lines similar to their own, in order that their ultimate aspirations for world peace may thus be realized. Accordingly the Governments of Germany, Italy and Japan have agreed as follows:

Article 1

Japan recognizes and respects the leadership of Germany and Italy in the establishment of a new order in Europe.

Article 2

Germany and Italy recognize and respect the leadership of Japan in the establishment of a new order in Greater East Asia.

Article 3

Germany, Italy and Japan agree to co-operate in their efforts on the aforesaid lines. They further undertake to assist one another with all political, economic and military means when one of the three Contracting Parties is attacked by a power at present not involved in the European War or in the Sino-Japanese Conflict.

Article 4

With a view to implementing the present Pact, Joint Technical Commissions the members of which are to be appointed by the respective Governments of Germany, Italy and Japan will meet without delay.

Article 5

Germany, Italy and Japan affirm that the aforesaid terms do not in any way affect the political status which exists at present as between each of the three Contracting Parties and Soviet Russia.

Article 6

The present Pact shall come into effect immediately upon signature and shall remain in force for ten years from the date of its coming into force.

At proper time before the expiration of the said term the High Contracting Parties shall, at the request of any one of them, enter into negotiations for its renewal.

In faith whereof, the Undersigned, duly authorized by

their respective Governments, have signed this Pact and have affixed hereto their Seals.

Done in triplicate at Berlin, the 27th day of September 1940—in the XVIIIth year of the Fascist Era—corresponding to the 27th day of the 9th month of the 15th year of Syowa.

Joachim v. Ribbentrop
Ciano
Kurusu

B. Strictly Confidential No. G. 1000 Tokyo, September 27, 1940.

Excellency: At the moment when our conversations on the Tripartite Pact, begun on the 9th of this month in Tokyo, are about to conclude successfully, it is Minister Stahmer's and my sincere desire to express to Your Excellency our deepest appreciation for the decisive part which you have played throughout in a most generous and accommodating spirit. We would like also to take this opportunity to state once more in this letter some of the most important points touched upon in our conversations.

The German Government is convinced that the contracting parties are about to enter a new and decisive phase of world history in which it will be their task to assume the leadership in the establishment of a new order in Greater East Asia and Europe respectively.

The fact that for a long time the interests of the contracting parties will be the same, together with their unlimited confidence in each other, forms the secure foundation for the Pact.

The German Government is firmly convinced that the technical details concerning the execution of the Pact can be settled without difficulties; it would not be in keeping with the far-reaching importance of the Pact, and would also not be practically possible, to try to regulate at the present time all the individual cases which may sometime come up. These questions can only be settled, instance by instance, in a spirit of intimate cooperation.

Conclusions of the Technical Commissions, provided for

in article 4 of the Pact should be submitted to the three Governments for approval in order to be put into force.

Needless to say, the question, whether an attack within the meaning of article 3 of the Pact has taken place, must be determined through joint consultation of the three contracting parties.

If Japan, contrary to the peaceful intent of the Pact, be attacked by a power so far not engaged in the European War or the China conflict, Germany will consider it a matter of course to give Japan full support and assist her with all military and economic means.

With regard to the relations between Japan and Soviet Russia, Germany will do everything within her power to promote a friendly understanding and will at any time offer her good offices to this end.

Germany will use her industrial strength and her other technical and material resources as far as possible in favor of Japan in order both to facilitate the establishment of a new order in Greater East Asia and to enable her to be better prepared for any emergency. Germany and Japan will further undertake to aid each other in procuring in every possible way necessary raw materials and minerals including oil.

The German Foreign Minister is firmly convinced that, if Italy's assistance and cooperation are sought in reference to the matters above enumerated, she will of course act in concord with Germany and Japan.

I have the honor to submit these statements to Your Excellency as the views of the German Foreign Minister conveyed personally by his special delegate, Minister Stahmer, and repeated also in instructions to me from my Government.

I avail myself of this opportunity to renew to Your Excellency the assurance of my highest consideration.

Ott

C. Strictly Confidential — Tokyo, September 27, 1940.
No. G. 1001

Excellency: I have the honor to acknowledge receipt of

Your Excellency's letter Jyo-ni[2] Nr. 133 of this date with contents as follows:

"I have the honor to inform Your Excellency that, the Japanese Government earnestly share the hope with the Governments of Germany and Italy that the present European War will remain limited as far as possible in its sphere and scope and will come to a speedy conclusion and that they shall on their part spare no effort in that direction.

"However, the conditions actually prevailing in Greater East Asia and elsewhere do not permit the Japanese Government to rest assured in the present circumstances that there is no danger whatever of an armed conflict taking place between Japan and Great Britain, and accordingly they desire to call attention of the German Covernment to such a possibility and to state that they feel confident that Germany will do their utmost to aid Japan in such eventuality with all means in their power."

I take this occasion to note the contents of Your Excellency's letter.

Accept, Mr. Minister, the renewed assurance of my highest consideration.

Ott

D. Strictly Confidential Tokyo, September 27, 1940.
No. G. 1002

Excellency: I have the honor to acknowledge receipt of Your Excellency's letter Jyo-ni Nr. 134 of this date and to confirm the oral declaration reproduced in it which I made concerning the former German colonies in the South Seas.

I avail myself of this opportunity to assure Your Excellency once more of my highest consideration.

Ott

E. Tr[eaty Department] September 27, 15th Year of Showa
2. [Section], No. 133
Strictly Confidential Absolutely Confidential

Excellency: I have the honour to inform Your Excellency

that the Japanese Government earnestly share the hope with the Government of Germany and Italy that the present European War will remain limited as far as possible in its sphere and scope and will come to a speedy conclusion and that they shall on their part spare no effort in that direction.

However, the conditions actually prevailing in Greater East Asia and elsewhere do not permit the Japanese Government to rest assured in the present circumstances that there is no danger whatever of an armed conflict taking place between Japan and Great Britain, and accordingly they desire to call attention of the German Government to such a possibility and to state that they feel confident that Germany will do their utmost to aid Japan in such eventuality with all means in their power.

I avail myself of this opportunity to renew to Your Excellency the highest consideration.

Yosuke Matsuoka

To the German Ambassador
Extraordinary and Plenipotentiary in Japan
His Excellency General Ott

F. Tr[eaty Department] September 27, 15th Year of Showa
2. [Section], No. 134
Strictly Confidential Absolutely Confidential

Excellency: I have the honour to ask Your Excellency to confirm the following oral declaration which was made by Your Excellency on behalf of the German Government:

"The German Government agree that the former German Colonies actually under Japan's Mandate in the South Seas shall remain in Japan's possession, it being understood that Germany be in a way compensated therefor. In regard to the other former Colonies in the South Seas, they shall be restored automatically to Germany upon conclusion of peace ending the present European War. Afterwards the German Government would be prepared to confer, in an accommodating spirit, with the Japanese Government with a view to disposing of them as far as possible in Japan's favor against compensation."

I avail myself of this opportunity to renew to Your Excellency the highest consideration.

Yosuke Matsuoka

To the German Ambassador
Extraordinary and Plenipotentiary in Tokyo
His Excellency General Ott

G. Tr[eaty Department] September 27, 15th Year of Showa
2. [Section], No. 135
Strictly Confidential Absolutely Confidential

Excellency: I have the honour to acknowledge receipt of Your Excellency's letter No. G 1000 of this date and I feel happy to take note of the contents therein.

I avail myself of this opportunity to renew to Your Excellency the highest consideration.

Yosuke Matsuoka

To the German Ambassador
Extraordinary and Plenipotentiary in Japan
His Excellency General Ott

Appendix 2

Military Agreement Between Germany, Italy, and Japan[1]

Top Secret

In the spirit of the Tripartite Pact of September 27, 1940, and in connection with the agreement of December 11, 1941, the German and the Italian Armed Forces and the Japanese Army and Navy herewith conclude a military agreement, in order to safeguard operational cooperation among them and to destroy the enemy's fighting strength as quickly as possible.

I. DIVISION OF ZONES OF OPERATION

The German and Italian Armed Forces and the Japanese Army and Navy will conduct the necessary operations within the zones assigned to them hereunder:

1. *Japan*

   a) the waters east of approximately 70 degrees eastern longitude to the west coast of the American continent, as well as the continents and islands (Australia, Dutch East Indies, New Zealand, etc.) which are located in these waters.

b) the Asian continent east of approximately 70 degrees eastern longitude.

2. *Germany and Italy*

a) the waters west of approximately 70 degrees eastern longitude to the east coast of the American continent, as well as the continents and islands (Africa, Iceland, etc.) which are located in these waters.

b) The Near East, the Middle East, and Europe west of approximately 70 degrees eastern longitude.

3. In the Indian Ocean, operations can be conducted across the agreed-upon zonal boundaries, depending on the situation.

II. GENERAL PLAN OF OPERATIONS

1. Japan, in cooperation with German and Italian operations against England and the United States of North America, will conduct operations in the area of the South Seas and in the Pacific.

a) She will destroy the important bases of England, the United States of North America, and Holland in Greater East Asia, and attack or occupy their territories located there.

b) She will aim at the destruction of the North American and English land, naval, and air forces in the Pacific Ocean and the Indian Ocean to gain command of the sea in the Western Pacific.

c) When the North American and English fleets are for the most part concentrated in the Atlantic, Japan will strengthen her war on enemy shipping [*Handelskrieg*] in the whole area of the Pacific and of the Indian Ocean and she will furthermore dispatch a part of her naval forces to the Atlantic to cooperate directly with the German and the Italian navies there.

2. Germany and Italy, in cooperation with Japanese operations in the South Seas and the Pacific, will carry

out operations against England and the United States of North America.

a) They will destroy important bases of England and the United States of North America in the Near and Middle East, in the Mediterranean and the Atlantic, and attack or occupy their territories located there.
b) They will aim at the destruction of the English and North American land, sea, and air forces in the Atlantic and the Mediterranean and the destruction of enemy shipping.
c) When the English and North American fleets are for the most part concentrated in the Pacific, Germany and Italy will dispatch a part of their naval forces to the Pacific to cooperate directly with the Japanese navy there.

III. MAIN POINTS OF MILITARY COOPERATION

1. Mutual contacts [*Fühlungname*] in regard to important points of operational planning.

2. Cooperation for purposes of the war against shipping, including
   a) mutual contact regarding planning for war on enemy shipping;
   b) mutual contacts regarding the course of the war on enemy shipping, important information, and other necessary details;
   c) if a partner intends to carry on war against enemy shipping outside the zone assigned to him, he will in advance notify the other partners so as to guarantee cooperation and mutual support in regard to the use of bases, supply, provisions, recreation of crews, repairs, etc.

3. Cooperation in regard to the collection and evaluation of information important for operations.

4. Cooperation in regard to military subversion.

5. Cooperation to safeguard military communications.

6. Cooperation to bring about a military air link be-

tween Germany, Italy and Japan, insofar as technical conditions allow, and to open sea connections and sea transport across the Indian Ocean.

In witness whereof the Chief of the Supreme Command of the German Armed Forces, the authorized representative of the Supreme Command of the Italian Armed Forces, and the authorized representatives of the Chief of the Imperial Japanese General Staff and of the Chief of the Imperial Japanese Naval Staff have signed this agreement. Done in the German, Italian, and Japanese language in Berlin, on the 18th of January 1942—in the XX year of the Fascist Era—which corresponds to the [18] day of the first month of the 17th year of the Era Showa.

Keitel
Marras
Nomura
Banzai

ABBREVIATIONS

DGFP	*Documents on German Foreign Policy* series
DNB	*Deutsches Nachrichten Büro*
GFM	German Foreign Ministry
IG	IG Farbenindustrie A.G.
IMT	International Military Tribunal, Nuremberg
IMTFE	International Military Tribunal for the Far East, Tokyo
IPS	International Prosecution Section (of IMTFE)
JFM	Japanese Foreign Ministry
NSR	*Nazi-Soviet Relations, 1939–1941*
NWD	Naval War Diary (*Kriegstagebuch der Seekriegsleitung*)
OCMH	Office of the Chief of Military History, United States Army
OKH	*Oberkommando des Heeres,* Supreme Command of the Army
OKM	*Oberkommando der Marine,* Supreme Command of the Navy
OKW	*Oberkommando der Wehrmacht,* Supreme Command of the Armed Forces
RdL	*Reichsministerium der Luftfahrt,* Reich Air Ministry
SEA	Staff Evidence Analysis (of an IMTFE or IMT document)
Skl	*Seekriegsleitung,* Navy Operations Staff
USNIP	*United States Naval Institute Proceedings*
USSBS	United States Strategic Bombing Survey
WiRüAmt	*Wehrwirtschafts- und Rüstungsamt,* Office of War Economy and Armaments, OKW

Notes

Notes to Chapter 1

1. Testimony of General Eugen Ott, German military attaché in Tokyo and later ambassador, on a conversation with Hitler in 1934. IMTFE, IPS File 324–9, p. 23.
2. See Gerhard L. Weinberg, "Die geheimen Abkommen zum Antikominternpakt," *Vierteljarhrshefte für Zeitgeschichte,* II (1954), 193–201.
3. "Minutes of the Conference in the Reich Chancellery, Berlin, November 5, 1937, from 4:15 to 8:30 P.M." (Hossbach Memorandum.) DGFP, (Washington: GPO, 1949–), Series D, Vol. I, pp. 29–39.
4. "Memorandum for the Führer," January 2, 1938. *Ibid.,* pp. 162–68.
5. Theo Sommer, *Deutschland und Japan zwischen den Mächten, 1935–1940* (Tübingen: Mohr, 1962), pp. 100–116. Germany recognized Manchukuo and withdrew aid and advisers from Chiang Kai-shek.
6. The negotiations are analyzed in Sommer, Chap. III, and in F. C. Jones, *Japan's New Order in East Asia: Its Rise and Fall, 1937–1945* (New York: Oxford University Press, 1954), Chap. IV.
7. Material in this paragraph is based on Jones, pp. 41, 57–70, 87, 102–03.
8. *Ibid.,* p. 88.

9. Berlin and Moscow were agreed on this point. See Gustav Hilger and Alfred G. Meyer, *The Incompatible Allies: German-Soviet Relations, 1918–1941* (New York: Macmillan, 1953), pp. 299, 307; and Raymond J. Sontag and James S. Beddie, eds., NSR (Washington: Department of State, 1948), pp. 57, 72–73.

10. For details, see Chapter 4 of the present book.

11. Memorandum by Unterstaatssekretär Ernst Woermann, October 8, 1939, initialed by Staatssekretär Ernst von Weizsäcker. DGFP, D, VIII, p. 243.

12. Jones, pp. 150–51, 153–54, 163–71.

13. Hubertus Lupke, *Japans Russlandpolitik von 1939 bis 1941* (Frankfurt: Metzner, 1962), pp. 73–76.

14. To supplement the Tokyo Trial record, which is very spotty, I have relied on the single best study of Japanese diplomacy at this time, Chihiro Hosoya, "Sankoku domei" [The Tripartite Pact] in Nihon Kokusai Seiji Gakkai, Taiheyo Senso Gen'in Kenkyubu, ed., *Taiheyo senso e no michi: kaisen gaiko shi* [The Road to the War in the Pacific: History of Foreign Relations on the Eve of the War] (Tokyo: Asahi, 1962–63), Vol. V. Professor James W. Morley, director of the East Asian Institute at Columbia University, who is editing the book for publication in English, has kindly lent me an English typescript translation. Footnote references are to the Japanese edition. For the attitude of the Yonai government and the army draft of late June, see pp. 175, 177, 179–80.

15. Hosoya, pp. 185–86, on the July 27 liaison conference and the Matsuoka draft of July 30.

16. On Hitler's strategic plans after the fall of France, see F. H. Hinsley, *Hitler's Strategy* (New York: Cambridge University Press, 1951); Helmuth Greiner, *Die oberste Wehrmachtführung, 1939–1943* (Wiesbaden: Limes-Verlag, 1951); and Alan Bullock, *Hitler: A Study in Tyranny*, rev. ed. (New York: Harper, 1962).

17. Testimony of Erich Kordt in United States of America versus Ernst von Weizsäcker et alii, German transcript of proceedings, mimeographed, p. 7472.

18. Jodl memorandum, "Die Weiterführung des Krieges gegen England," June 30, 1940. IMT, Doc. PS-1776.

19. *Halder Diary* (Washington: Infantry Journal, 1947). On Hitler's plans vis-à-vis Russia, see Gerhard L. Weinberg, *Germany and the Soviet Union, 1939–1941* (Leiden: Brill, 1954), and George E. Blau, *The German Campaign in Russia: Planning and Operations, 1940–1942* (Washington: Department of the Army, 1955).

20. Witness the American-Canadian defense agreement of mid-August and the bases-destroyer deal of early September.

21. Hosoya, pp. 194–95, 197–98, contains a detailed discussion of Japanese internal deliberations on which I have drawn for this and the following paragraph.

22. Stahmer and Ott admitted as much. See IMTFE, IPS File 244–35, pp. 16–17, and IPS File 324–20, pp. 3–4.

23. See for instance *The New York Times* and *New York Herald Tribune*, September 28, 1940, and *Time*, October 7, 1940. Similarly Winston Churchill, who suspected secret clauses, so unfavorable did the public pact seem to Japan. *Blood, Sweat, and Tears* (New York: Putnam's, 1941), p. 390.

24. Hosoya, pp. 202–04; and Johanna M. Menzel, "Der geheime deutsch-japanische Notenaustausch zum Dreimächtepakt," *Vierteljahrshefte für Zeitgeschichte*, V (1957), 182–93.

25. Stahmer, who promised to inform Berlin on his return, failed to do so (Menzel, p. 187, note 20). The Japanese remained under the impression, conveyed by the letters themselves, that Ribbentrop stood behind the secret annexes. See interrogation of Shunichi Matsumoto, head of the treaty bureau in the JFM, IMTFE, IPS File 247–69.

26. See Chapter 3 of the present book.

27. Winston Churchill, *Their Finest Hour* (Boston: Houghton Mifflin, 1949), p. 337; Ronald Wheatley, *Operation Sealion: German Plans for the Invasion of England, 1939–1942* (Oxford: Clarendon Press, 1958), pp. 88–90.

28. Molotov's statement on November 13, 1940, NSR, p. 247.

29. IMTFE, IPS Doc. 1285, p. 8.

30. For details, see Lupke, pp. 98–101, 119–26, and Toshikazu Kase, *Journey to the Missouri* (New Haven: Yale University Press, 1950), pp. 155–58.

31. Maurice Matloff and Edwin M. Snell, *Strategic Planning for Coalition Warfare, 1941–1942* (Washington: GPO, 1953), Chap. II, especially pp. 25–31.

32. Hitler conference with Admiral Erich Raeder, December 27, 1940. *Fuehrer Conferences on Matters Dealing with the German Navy, 1939–1945* (Washington: Department of the Navy, 1947), 1940, Vol. II, p. 69. Also Ott to GFM, January 31, 1941. DGFP, D, XI, pp. 1231–33.

33. *Fuehrer Conferences,* 1941, I, pp. 12–19.

34. "Über Zusammenarbeit mit Japan," IMT, Doc. PS-384.

35. Conversation with the Japanese ambassador, Hiroshi Oshima, and instructions to Ott, February 23 and 27, 1941. IMT, Doc. PS-1834 and DGFP, D, XII, p. 183.

36. Hitler-Raeder conference, January 8–9, 1941. *Fuehrer Conferences,* 1941, I, p. 4. In fact, the United States did not commit itself to the defense of Singapore at this time. See Matloff and Snell, pp. 34–38.

37. On the views of OKW, see Greiner, pp. 374–75.

38. Takushiro Hattori, *Dai toa senso zenshi* [The Complete History of the Greater East Asia War] (Tokyo: Masu Shobo, 1953–56), Vol. I, Part I, pp. 90–91. Page references are based on an English typescript translation, kindly made available by Professor Louis Morton, formerly of the Office of the Chief of Military History, United States Army.

39. Conversations of Matsuoka and the German leaders in NSR, pp. 376–83, 386–94, 405–09, 413–20, 453–58, 469–74.

40. Konoye memoir, "Facts about the Tripartite Alliance," IMTFE, IPS Doc. 849, p. 7.

41. Report by General Alfred Kretschmer, German military

attaché in Tokyo, cited in Major-General Burkhart Müller-Hillebrand, "Die militärische Zusammenarbeit Deutschlands und seiner Verbündeten während des zweiten Weltkrieges," unpublished manuscript in OCMH, "German Staff Studies," No. P-108, p. 330.

42. Joachim von Ribbentrop, *Zwischen London und Moskau: Erinnerungen und letzte Aufzeichnungen* (Leoni am Starnberger See: Druffel, 1953), p. 248; see also Chapter 5 of the present book.

43. On the significance of the Siberian route, see statistics in T. H. Vail Motter, *The Persian Corridor and Aid to Russia* (Washington: GPO, 1952).

44. The following is based on Hattori, I, I, pp. 78–131.

45. On the American decision and its background, see Herbert Feis, *The Road to Pearl Harbor* (Princeton: Princeton University Press, 1950), Chaps. XXIX–XXXI.

46. The documentary record is in United States Department of State, *Papers Relating to the Foreign Relations of the United States: Japan, 1931–1941* (Washington: GPO, 1943).

47. Japan's minimum demands are in her notes of November 1941. Before the July embargo, they had been stiffer.

48. Konoye memoir on Japanese-American relations, IMTFE, IPS Doc. 570, pp. 31–35. Differences of policy vis-à-vis Russia between Matsuoka and his colleagues were only a secondary element in Matsuoka's ouster.

49. The Japanese position and American responses are in *Foreign Relations: Japan*, II, pp. 593, 613, 709, 716, 724, covering the period from September through early November 1941. See also Paul W. Schroeder, *The Axis Alliance and Japanese-American Relations* (Ithaca: Cornell University Press, 1958), Chap. IV.

50. Ribbentrop to Ott, May 11, 1941. DGFP, D, XII, p. 778.

51. Ott to GFM, May 12, 1941 (*Ibid.*, p. 794). Later German complaints about being left in the dark are in Ott to GFM, July 10, 1941 (*Ibid.*, XIII, pp. 108–10).

52. Ott to GFM, May 14, 1941 (*Ibid.*, XII, pp. 806–10), and Ribbentrop to Ott, May 15, 1941 (*Ibid.*, pp. 820–22).

53. *Ibid.*

54. Ribbentrop to Ott, May 11, 1941. *Ibid.*, pp. 777–80.

55. Compare Matsuoka's statement to Ott (Ott to Ribbentrop, May 15, 1941, DGFP, D, XII, pp. 818–19) and to Ambassador Joseph Grew (Grew, *Ten Years in Japan* [New York: Simon & Schuster, 1944], p. 389). According to Grew's report to the State Department, Matsuoka spoke more toughly. *Foreign Relations: Japan,* II, pp. 145–48.

56. On FDR's motives see Robert E. Sherwood, *Roosevelt and Hopkins* (New York: Harper, 1948), pp. 298–99.

57. Ribbentrop to Ott, July 10, 1941. DGFP, D, XIII, pp. 110–13.

58. Ribbentrop to Ott, September, 14. *Ibid.*, p. 505.

59. Ott to GFM, September 20 and 26, 1941. *Ibid.*, pp. 537–38 and 569–70. On Ott's conversation with Eiji Amau, deputy foreign minister, on October 2, see IMTFE, IPS Doc. 3121–(2), SEA. For Grew's talk with Amau, October 15, see *Foreign Relations: Japan,* II, pp. 686.

60. On November 12, Secretary of State Cordell Hull remarked to the Japanese ambassador, "The matter of the Tripartite Pact relationship ought not to be a problem if we could work out our proposed arrangement in other ways." *Foreign Relations: Japan,* II, p. 724.

61. Remarks by Foreign Minister Toyoda, reported in Ott to GFM, September 13, 1941. DGFP, D, XIII, pp. 490–93. See also *Nippon Times,* September and early October, for comments on the slowdown of the German offensive.

62. Ott to Ribbentrop, October 4, 1941. DGFP, D, XIII, pp. 608–11. Also interrogation of Kretschmer, IMTFE, IPS File 324–62, p. 16.

63. *Halder Diary,* October 8. Indirect evidence for German confidence is in Burton Klein, *Germany's Economic Preparation for War* (Cambridge: Harvard University Press, 1959), p. 192.

64. IMTFE, IPS Doc. 790.

65. The best synopsis of American policy is in Donald F.

Drummond, *The Passing of American Neutrality, 1937–1941* (Ann Arbor: University of Michigan Press, 1955); of German policy in Hans L. Trefousse, *Germany and American Neutrality, 1939–1941* (New York: Bookman, 1951).

66. OKM to OKW, December 2, 1941. NWD.

67. OKM, memorandum of December 8, 1941. NWD.

68. For the date, see Oshima's dispatch to JFM, December 8, 1941, in United States, 79th Congress, Joint Committee on the Investigation of the Pearl Harbor Attack, *Hearings* (Washington: GPO, 1946), Part 12, Exhibit 1, p. 253. The directive was discussed in OKM on December 9. NWD.

69. *Pearl Harbor Hearings, loc. cit.*

70. OKM pointed out to OKW on December 8 that the new directive created a *de facto* state of war with the United States and that neutrals should be informed of the new German procedures. See OKM memo, December 8, 1941, NWD. Had a declaration of war seemed imminent the recommended warning to the neutrals would of course have been pointless.

71. Oshima to JFM, December 5, 1941. *Pearl Harbor Hearings,* Part 35, Exhibit 148, pp. 684–85. The German promise of December 5 had Hitler's sanction but was almost certainly made without any realization of how soon Japan intended to strike.

72. For this and further details, see Trefousse, "Germany and Pearl Harbor," *Far Eastern Quarterly,* XI (1951), 35–50.

73. For German evaluations of this material, see a folder marked "Roosevelt Plan für Grossoffensive gegen Europa," NWD.

74. NWD, December 11, 1941.

75. Text of Roosevelt speech in *The New York Times,* December 10, 1941.

76. On December 9, a spokesman of the Japanese government publicly called on Germany to declare war on the United States. DNB dispatch from Tokyo, IMTFE, IPS Doc. 4071, Item 15.

77. This reconstruction of German estimates is based on

post-December 11 materials. See below, Chapter 2. It is assumed that the German services came to very much the same conclusion in their attempts between December 7 and 11 to predict American strategy in a hypothetical two-front war.

Notes to Chapter 2

1. *Fuehrer Conferences,* 1941, I, pp. 18–19.
2. Robert E. Ward, "The Inside Story of the Pearl Harbor Plan," *United States Naval Institute Proceedings,* LXXVII (1951), 1271–83.
3. "Liaison Conference Decision Plan, November 11, 1941," IMTFE, IPS Doc. 1444.
4. The Japanese had made only vague suggestions for joint operations in the Indian Ocean when they urged a negotiated settlement with Russia in October 1941.
5. His colleague in Rome felt that "Oshima was a soldier and blindly followed the German generals." See a German evaluation of captured Italian documents in GFM Files, Serial 131, Frames 70822–25.
6. To make up for Oshima's unrealistic reporting, the Japanese sent a mission to Germany in the spring of 1943. See Stahmer to GFM, and memorandum by Counsellor of Legation Gottfriedsen, May 13, 1943. GFM Files /27/ 17210–11.
7. See Charles A. Willoughby, *Shanghai Conspiracy: The Sorge Spy Ring* (New York: Dutton, 1952) and Chalmers Johnson, *An Instance of Treason: Ozaki Hotsumi and the Sorge Spy Ring* (Stanford: Stanford University Press, 1964). Ott's defense of his relation to Sorge is in Ott to GFM, March 29, 1942, GFM Files /60/39967 ff.
8. For details of the project, see NWD, August 19, October 19 and 31, November 2 and 5, 1942. Also GFM Files /1027 /310071–140 and /929/297742–43.
9. Yale C. Maxon, *Control of Japanese Foreign Policy: A Study of Civil-Military Rivalry, 1930–1945* (Berkeley:

University of California Press, 1957), pp. 61–62, and Hattori, I, II, p. 240.

10. For Hitler's military decision-making, see Bullock, pp. 719–20. On the insignificance of single-service studies, see Erich von Manstein, *Lost Victories* (Chicago: Regnery, 1958), p. 54.

11. Minutes of the first of these talks, on August 5, 1942, in NWD. A hand-written marginal comment pointedly remarks: "First military discussion after Japan's entry into the war on December 7, 1941!"

12. Specifically, liaison was established between the German naval staff and the Japanese member of the Tripartite military committee in Berlin, Admiral Naokuni Nomura, who appeared about once a month at the naval high command, accompanied by the military attaché. Some liaison functions also fell to Admiral Otto Groos, the German member of the Tripartite military committee and concurrently head of a special OKW office for war on enemy shipping and economic warfare (*Sonderstab HWK: Handelskrieg und wirtschaftliche Kampfmassnahmen*).

13. IMT, Doc. PS-3776.

14. The signatures of two Japanese, one signing for the army, one for the navy, point to the split in the supreme command referred to above.

15. Prior notification took place whenever Japanese submarines or German auxiliary cruisers operated in their ally's operational zone. Only minor frictions developed over these arrangements. See NWD, *passim.*

16. Whether cooperation in intelligence matters was very effective may be doubted. In pre-Pearl Harbor days there was little of it. The Germans who knew that the United States had broken the Japanese code seem not to have informed Tokyo. See Counsellor Hans Thomsen (Washington) to GFM, April 28, 1941. DGFP, D, XII, p. 661.

17. Germany, with few heavy surface ships, concentrated on submarine warfare against enemy merchant shipping. Japan, with a battle fleet and naval air arm, sought encounters between fleets.

18. NWD, December 7 and 11, 1941, and memoranda of the naval staff, OKW and OKH, between December 1941 and March 1942, filed in NWD.

19. Richard M. Leighton and Robert W. Coakley, *Global Logistics and Strategy, 1940–1943* (Washington: GPO, 1955), p. 353. The rest of the paragraph is based on Matloff and Snell, *passim;* especially pp. 162–63, 175–79.

20. "Denkschrift der Seekriegsleitung zur Frage: welche strategischen Forderungen ergeben sich aus der gegenwärtigen Lage für die weitere Kriegführung der Dreierpaktmächte," NWD.

21. "Sobald eine derartige Zielsetzung der Achsenmächte zur Unterbrechung der britischen Land- und Seeverbindung Mittelmeer-Mittlerer Osten/Indien erkennbar ist, wird Japan mit aller Energie zur Erkämpfung der Seeherrschaft im Indischen Ozean/Persischen Golf antreten." *Ibid.*

22. The approval is recorded in NWD, March 9, 1942.

23. *Ibid.*, March 27, 1942.

24. Minutes of the Hitler-Mussolini meeting, April 30, 1942, in GFM Files /67/47798–800.

25. See Jodl diary, May 7, 20, 21, 1942. IMT, Doc. PS-1807.

26. NWD. A similar entry is under February 17, 1942.

27. Führer directive No. 41, April 5, 1942. *Fuehrer Directives and Other Top-Level Directives of the German Armed Forces* (Washington: Department of the Navy, 1948), mimeographed.

28. Halder's comment in NWD, April 8, 1942.

29. On the Ceylon data, see NWD, February 10 and 21, 1942. Raeder presented the gist of the navy memorandum of February 25 to Hitler as early as February 13. Nomura's warning came on February 10 in a conversation with Groos. See NWD, February 25, 1942.

30. *Ibid.*, February 20 and March 6, 1942.

31. Japanese newspaper articles are mentioned in the NWD, February 13 and 16, and Tojo's speech on February 16, 1942.

32. Kurt Assmann, *Deutsche Schicksalsjahre* (Wiesbaden: Brockhaus, 1950), p. 356.

33. Mitsuo Fuchida and Masatake Okumiya, *Midway: The Battle that Doomed Japan* (Annapolis: United States Naval Institute, 1955), pp. 48–49.

34. Hattori, II, II, pp. 115–17. While critical of the navy's "adventurism," Colonel Hattori provides a factual and detailed account of navy plans and army-navy deliberations. The role of the Combined Fleet and its strategic planning within the naval staff are more clearly described by Fuchida and Okumiya.

35. Fuchida and Okumiya, p. 49.

36. *Ibid.*, pp. 49–50.

37. *Ibid.*, p. 51.

38. Fuchida and Okumiya provide few dates, but their account suggests that the Combined Fleet first considered the offensive in the Indian Ocean in early February.

39. Fuchida and Okumiya, pp. 51–52.

40. I have not been able to pinpoint the origin of the Japanese draft for a military agreement. In presenting it in Berlin, Admiral Nomura insisted it was chiefly for domestic political consumption. NWD, December 17, 1941.

41. Ribbentrop to Ott, March 18, 1942. IMTFE, IPS Doc. 4033, Item 13. Ribbentrop virtually invited the Japanese to Madagascar, even while insisting that for Germany the Russian theater would remain paramount.

42. NWD, February 17, 1942.

43. Ott to Ribbentrop, March 2, 1942. IMTFE, IPS Doc. 4033, Item 12.

44. Ribbentrop to Ott, March 8, 1942. GFM Files /50/ 33012–14.

45. Fuchida and Okumiya, p. 52.

46. *Ibid.*, p. 53.

47. Such Japanese fears were reported by Ott to GFM, January 27, 1942. IMTFE, IPS Doc. 11-A (7). The parallel to China must have been obvious.

48. On the briefing of the Japanese, see NWD, March 20, 1942.

49. Fuchida and Okumiya, p. 65. According to Hattori, II, III, p. 132, the Midway project had already been advanced by the Combined Fleet in early March.

50. Hattori, II, III, pp. 124–25 on the planning background. On the operation, see Stanley Woodburn Kirby, *The War Against Japan*. Vol. II, *India's Most Dangerous Hour* (London: HMSO, 1958), Chap. VII.

51. Fuchida and Okumiya, pp. 63–72; Hattori, II, III, pp. 130 ff.

52. NWD, May 2 and 15, 1942.

53. The Japanese position is set forth in NWD, May 21, and in Ott/Kretschmer to OKH, August 28, 1942. GFM Files /1027/310196–99. The German position is in NWD, June 27, 1942.

54. On the revival of Japanese hopes, see Hattori, II, II, pp. 156–57; Ott/Wennecker to OKM/OKW, July 2, and Ott to GFM, July 7, 1942, GFM Files /21/13366–67 and /13380–83. Paul Wennecker was the German naval attaché.

55. NWD, instructions to Wennecker, July 8, and records of conversation with Nomura, June 22 and August 5, the latter in OKW.

56. NWD, July 3, 1942. The German navy did not credit American claims to have sunk four Japanese carriers at Midway, and the Japanese did not admit their losses to the Germans, it seems. NWD, June 25 and July 15, 1942.

57. NWD, August 11, 1942.

58. Jodl-Nomura conversations, August 5 and October 16, 1942, NWD. In October, Jodl suggested that German operations beyond the Caucasus had to be postponed to 1943. For Hitler's view in September, see notes by the OKW war diarist in OCMH, German Staff Studies, Greiner Series, MS #C-065-a, entry September 8.

59. Nomura talk with, and letter to, naval staff, November 20 and 21, 1942. NWD.

60. NWD, November 30, 1942.

61. Situation report (*Lagebericht*) of OKM, December 11, 1942. NWD.

62. OKW situation report of December 10, 1942, in NWD.

63. The attaché's dispatch and Jodl's reprimand of December 24, 1942, in NWD.

64. Admiral Fricke in a conversation with Nomura, January 22, 1943. NWD.

Notes to Chapter 3

1. While Japan had asked the belligerents to express respect for the *status quo* of the Dutch East Indies, Germany alone had gone further and declared herself disinterested. Publicly, Japan hailed this as a German *carte blanche,* while privately the government continued to suspect German designs on the islands. See interministerial conference of July 16, 1940, IMTFE, IPS Doc. 1392, pp. 2–3. Nor were all Germans happy about the government statement.

2. See record of Stahmer's initial meetings with Matsuoka, IMTFE, IPS Doc. 1129. Stahmer seems not to have inquired about the size of Greater East Asia.

3. Document compilation by Shunichi Matsumoto, IMTFE, Def. Doc. 1656, read into English transcript of proceedings, p. 27990.

4. On Hitler's possible terms with England in late June or early July, see Hinsley, p. 81; Bullock, pp. 588–89.

5. Navy plans in *Fuehrer Conferences,* 1940, I, pp. 65–66. The whole issue of German colonial plans has been dealt with by Gerhard L. Weinberg, "German Colonial Plans and Policies, 1938–1942," in *Geschichte und Gegenwartsbewusstsein: Festschrift für Hans Rothfels* (Göttingen: Vandenhoeck & Ruprecht, 1963), pp. 462–91.

6. *Halder Diary,* July 13, 1940.

7. Berlin had, on the one hand, ordered an end to French demobilization in Indo-China, yet on the other prevented reinforcements from reaching the colony. The prospect of reinforcements was dangled before the French all summer

and then abruptly withdrawn on September 20, when Stahmer's talks in Tokyo were well advanced. Details are in the memoirs of Vichy personnel and in *La délégation française auprès de la Commission Allemande d'Armistice: recueil de documents* (Paris: Costes, 1947), *passim.*

8. Ribbentrop to Embassy Paris, February 23, 1941 (IMTFE, IPS Doc. 3364), advising France to accept Japanese mediation. In the July crisis, German pressure on Vichy was presumably less strong, because Berlin at the time sought Vichy's cooperation with German supply plans in Africa. Still, there must have been some support for Japan, because Tokyo gave thanks. Ott to GFM, July 24, 1941, DGFP, D, XIII, pp. 208–209.

9. IMTFE, IPS Doc. 1129.

10. Details of the Franco-German agreement and its sequel of January 1941 are in "Tätigkeitsbericht der deutschen Waffenstillstandsdelegation für Wirtschaft, Wiesbaden," for the July-December 1940 and January-June 1941 periods, IMT, Docs. PS-1986 and 1987. These agreements were in conflict with the Franco-Japanese treaty of August 30, 1940, under which Japan had received preferential status in Indo-China vis-à-vis third powers.

11. "Aufzeichnung betr. Wirtschaftsbeziehungen mit Japan," November 15, 1940, by Emil Wiehl, head of the GFM's economic division, DGFP, D, XI, pp. 583–86. Also Ott to GFM, January 23, 1941, IMTFE, IPS Doc. 4032, Item 11.

12. Wiehl to Ott, December 2, 1940. DGFP, D, XI, p. 745, note 2.

13. Wiehl to Ott, January 22, 1941. *Ibid.*, p. 1161.

14. Memorandum by Dr. Helmuth Wohlthat, leader of a forthcoming German economic mission to Japan, March 28, 1941. IMTFE, IPS Doc. 4038, Item 47.

15. Article 9 of the first secret protocol to the German-Japanese treaty of economic cooperation of January 20, 1940. National Archives, World War II Records Division (Alexandria, Va.), OKW, WiRüAmt Folder Wi/VI. 183.

16. Memoranda by Weizsäcker and Woermann on talks with members of the Japanese embassy, June 7 and 11, 1940.

GFM Files /173/84366–67, and IMTFE, IPS Doc. 4027, Item 4. The Japanese views are reported in Ott to GFM, February 4, 1941, IMTFE, IPS Doc. 4037, Item 5.

17. Hitler's views, described in a memorandum of June 12, 1940. GFM Files /173/84372–75. Seyss-Inquart's article was originally a talk to the Auslands-Organisation of the party in The Hague.

18. *Halder Diary,* October 15, 1940.

19. *Ibid.,* November 16, 1940.

20. Weizsäcker memorandum to Ribbentrop, March 24, 1941. DGFP, D, XII, pp. 348–49. This is further proof that the highest echelons of the GFM had no knowledge of the secret annexes to the Tripartite Pact in which the former German islands had already been promised to Japan.

21. Sommer, p. 438.

22. Ribbentrop to Ott, January 1, 1942. IMTFE, IPS Doc. 4075, Item 1. On the party's dilemma vis-à-vis Mussert, see Counsellor Behne (The Hague) to GFM, March 9, 1942. GFM Files /173/84464–65.

23. Behne to GFM, January 31, 1942. *Ibid.,* /84460–61.

24. Behne to GFM, March 9, 1942. *Ibid.,* /84464–65.

25. Details in Jones, pp. 92–98.

26. For the German demand, see Matsumoto document compilation, IMTFE, Def. Doc. 1656, English transcript of proceedings, pp. 27987 and 28005. The German formula was dropped in the final version; see Appendix One.

27. According to a Japanese fascicle of documents, "Collection of treaties, agreements, documents exchanged, concerning restitution of concessions and abolition of extraterritoriality in China during 1943," IMTFE, IPS Doc. 1497, SEA. This takeover had not yet been implemented by the late summer, because the Japanese occupied the Italian concession in Tientsin and disarmed Italian troops in China only at the time of Badoglio's surrender. See Stahmer to GFM, September 9, 1943. GFM Files /27/17368–69.

28. IMTFE, IPS Doc. 1497, SEA. The analyst's commentary to item 18 mentions German pressure on Vichy.

29. Premier Kuniaki Koiso's statement to the Diet, reported in *Osaka Mainichi*, March 12, 1945.

30. Japanese awareness of the German point of view in Ott to GFM, February 21 and 23, 1942. GFM Files /60/39702, and IMTFE, IPS Doc. 4076, Item 8.

31. Study by the Cabinet Planning Board's Total War Research Institute, February 1942. IMTFE, IPS Doc. 1021-C.

32. Ott to GFM, November 12, 1942, and Woermann memoranda of November 28 and December 5, 1942, GFM Files /929/297678 and /297779–80 and /1028/310357–58; also a Weizsäcker memorandum of November 27, 1942, /853 /284768–69.

33. NSR, pp. 221–2, 250, 257. Japanese ideas are reported in Ott to Ribbentrop, November 11, 1940, IMTFE, IPS Doc. 4042, Item 38. Japan was ready to throw in Outer Mongolia and Sinkiang for good measure.

34. "Entwurf zu einer militärischen Vereinbarung zwischen Japan, Deutschland und Italien," GFM Files /1029/ 310483–86.

35. Woermann to Weizsäcker, December 26, 1941, and latter's marginal comments. *Ibid.*, /310572–73.

36. OKM to Groos, December 19, 1941. *Ibid.*, /310585–87.

37. WiRüAmt to Groos, December 23, 1941. *Ibid.*, /310583–84.

38. "Stichworte für eine Unterredung des GFM Keitel mit Nomura (und Banzai) *nach* der Unterzeichnung, am besten bei dem Frühstück." *Ibid.*, /310521–22.

39. Staff memorandum for Ribbentrop, "Für den Vortrag beim Führer über die militärische Vereinbarung mit Japan," December 30, 1941. *Ibid.*, /310545–47.

40. Ott to GFM, March 5, 1942. *Ibid.*, /60/39767–68.

41. *Ibid.*, /3179/D693387-91 and /D694109.

42. Correspondence between GFM and Embassy Rome (Quirinal), *Ibid.*, /978/303468–97. The idea for such a

declaration had come from the Italians in January; they, Ribbentrop, and Bose now welcomed the Japanese proposal, but Hitler vetoed it, on the grounds that a commitment to the Indians and Arabs might obstruct a possible separate peace with Britain. Hitler-Mussolini meeting, April 29, 1942. *Ibid.*, /67/47767–97.

43. *Ibid.*, Serials 60 and 978, *passim*.

44. Eventually the Indian units were used on the quieter sectors of the Western front, after the Allied invasion of France.

45. Bose-Hitler talk, May 28, 1942, GFM Files /67/47826–40. Hitler made it clear that India could not count on German support in defining her eastern border against "Greater East Asia."

46. The Germans helped spirit Bose to East Asia. See Captain Musenberg, "Unbekannter Passagier auf U-180," *Der Frontsoldat erzählt*, XIX (1955), pp. 181–82. In November 1943, Germany recognized Bose's new government, established under Japanese patronage. GFM Files /27/17445–46.

47. Woermann memorandum for Ribbentrop, April 17, 1942 (GFM Files /50/33067), advocating Japanese ties to Raschid Ali el Gailani. As early as the spring of 1941, Berlin had tried to get Japanese arms for him. IMT, Doc. NG-94. In February 1941 Berlin had advocated Japanese arms aid for Ibn Saud, while Italy opposed strengthening Arab states. GFM Files /833/280740–43.

48. On the Japanese approach, see Ott/Wennecker to OKM, February 19, 1942, and Ott to GFM, February 20, 1942. *Ibid.*, /60/39694–96.

49. GFM to Ott, February 7, 1942. *Ibid.*, /39726–28.

50. NWD, March 2, 1942.

51. NWD, March 6; and Hitler-Raeder conference, March 12, 1942, in *Fuehrer Conferences*, 1942, pp. 18–19.

52. *Ibid.*, p. 19.

53. Ribbentrop to Ott, March 18, 1942, on his recent but undated conversation with Oshima. IMTFE, IPS Doc. 4033, Item 13.

54. Vichy's requests to Japan are mentioned in Jodl diary, April 28, 1942 (IMT, Doc. PS-1807), and in Ribbentrop-Ciano conference, April 29, 1942 (GFM Files /67/47762–66). On May 9, Oshima confirmed that France had sought aid which Japan, however, was forced to decline (*Ibid.*, /48288–96).

55. A Japanese request was presented on May 13, 1942. NWD.

56. Privy Council meeting, October 1, 1941, IMTFE, IPS Doc. 1169, SEA. The German request had been made in August, and presumably earlier. See Ott to GFM, August 6, 1941, IMTFE, IPS Doc. 4064.

57. German evaluation of captured Italian documents, where Italo-Japanese advocacy of greater rights for Europe's small nations is noted. GFM Files /131/70822–25.

58. Oshima pursued this idea in August 1942, February 1943, and September 1943, and Foreign Minister Mamoru Shigemitsu did so in December 1943. See GFM Files /853 /284760; /50/33581; /27/17375–78; and /17498–99.

59. Ribbentrop's remark to Oshima, cited in instructions to Stahmer, May 25, 1943. *Ibid.*, /27/17248–52.

Notes to Chapter 4

1. Ernst L. Presseisen, *Germany and Japan: A Study in Totalitarian Diplomacy, 1933–1941* (The Hague: Nijhoff, 1958), p. 227.

2. W. N. Medlicott, *The Economic Blockade* (London: HMSO, 1952, 1959), Vol. I, Chap. XI. I am much indebted to this book for material in this chapter.

3. Ott to GFM, April 17, 1940. IMTFE, IPS Doc. 4030, Item 24.

4. My calculations are based on data in Medlicott and in League of Nations, *International Trade Statistics: 1938* (Geneva: The League, 1939) and on a memo by OKW, WiRüAmt, "Die Wehrwirtschaft Mandschukuos, Stand August 1940," September 15, 1940, National Archives, Microcopy T-82, Roll 92, Frames 248452 ff.

5. NSR, pp. 109, 133.

6. OKW, WiRüAmt, "Der wirtschaftliche Aufbau des 'Fernen Ostens' und seine Bedeutung für die deutsche Wehrwirtschaft," September 1940, Microcopy T-82/92/248786 ff. Also an IG Farben report of May 17, 1940 on German trade with Manchuria. IMT, Doc. NI-1096.

7. WiRüAmt memo, as in note 6.

8. OKW, WiRüAmt, "Kautschuk und die Versorgungslage im Kriege," March 1941. Microcopy T-77/346/1184600 ff. On synthetic rubber production, see also a post-war IG Farben memo in IMT, Doc. NI-10026.

9. On German stockpiling and technical progress in steel manufacture, see Burton Klein, Table 15 and pp. 118–21.

10. Ott to GFM, April 17, 1940, IMTFE, IPS Doc. 4030, Item 24. Similarly, Wiehl to Weizsäcker, June 24, 1940, IPS Doc. 4025-B.

11. The following paragraphs are based primarily on two "Tätigkeitsberichte der deutschen Waffenstillstandsdelegation für Wirtschaft," covering the period from June 1940 to June 1941 (IMT, Docs. PS-1986 and 1987) and on a number of documents from the Tokyo trial.

12. Medlicott, II, pp. 89–96.

13. Figures on goods in transit were given by Stalin to the British and are reproduced in Medlicott, I, Appendix III (ii).

14. Medlicott, II, pp. 102–103.

15. Cheng Yu-kwei, *Foreign Trade and Industrial Development of China* (Washington, D.C.: University Press of Washington, D.C., 1956), pp. 131–33.

16. IMT, Doc. PS-1987. On French commitments to Japan, see Medlicott, II, pp. 95–96.

17. Record of a conversation between Generals Keitel and Jodl and General Kurt Thomas, head of WiRüAmt, February 8, 1941, IMT, Doc. PS-1456. See also General Thomas' memorandum, "Die wehrwirtschaftlichen Auswirkungen einer Operation im Osten," IMT, Doc. PS-2353, pp. 364–66.

18. Medlicott, I, p. 429.
19. For data in this paragraph, see Ott and Wohlthat dispatches to GFM, December 20, 1941, and July 10, 1942. IMTFE, IPS Doc. 4067; GFM Files /21/13389–91. Also Wohlthat interrogation, IMTFE, IPS File 334–5.
20. "German blockade breakers between Japan and Western France from the beginning of the war until the end of December 1943," in the files of USSBS, National Archives, RG 243, Section II, Item 54 nn(8). Very similar figures are in "Opium, Erz und Öle," *Der Frontsoldat erzählt*, XVIII, No. 8 (1954), pp. 246–47.
21. *Ibid.*, p. 246.
22. Difficulties are analyzed in a memorandum by Groos, June 5, 1943, "Der Warenaustausch mit Ostasien im Verschiffungszeitraum 1942/43," NWD. On the end of surface shipping, see OKW, WStb(Ausl)2/I "Nachtrag zur Vortragsnotiz vom 17.2," February 19, 1944, in National Archives, World War II Records Division (Alexandria, Va.), OKW, WiRüAmt Folder Wi/II c. 3.4.
23. USSBS report, National Archives, RG 243, Section II, Item 54nn(8).
24. Groos to Keitel, OKW L 23 HWK Nr. 113/43 gKdos, February 23, 1943, in OKW, WiRüAmt Folder Wi/II c. 3.3.
25. Exchange of correspondence between German and Japanese navies, June–August 1943. NWD.
26. On the fate of the Japanese boats, see interrogations of Japanese officers, USSBS, National Archives, RG 243, Section II, Item 54 nn(7). On the German and Italian boats, "Opium, Erz und Öle," p. 247.
27. Medlicott, II, p. 452.
28. Remark by a general staff representative at a three-ministers conference, July 16, 1940. IMTFE, IPS Doc. 1392, p. 5.
29. *Ibid.;* statement by Mr. Ando from JFM.
30. For cabinet decision and subsequent missions, see IMTFE, IPS Doc. 1308, and GFM Files /1671/394608–10.

31. Interrogation of Captain Tadao Yokoi, Japanese naval attaché in Berlin, IMTFE, IPS File 247–79. Also OKW, WiRüAmt, "Kurze Übersicht der Wehrwirtschaft Japans," March 1941, in Microcopy T-82/92/248432 ff.

32. NWD, February 11, 1941. And WiRüAmt Stab Ia to Colonel Hünermann, No. 158 of February 22, 1941, which complains that "Japan maintains dozens of commissions in Germany which really only snoop around [*herumschnüffeln*]." Microcopy T-77/334/1170329.

33. For views of Friedrich Krupp Werke and Zeiss, see IMT, Doc. NI-10201, letter of February 1941.

34. Quoted in Greiner, p. 275.

35. *Ibid.*, p. 376.

36. OKW, WiRüAmt, "Aktennotiz: Betr. Besuch Herr Sakai vom Büro des Jap. Marineattaché," February 2, 1943. OKW, WiRüAmt Folder Wi/II c.3.3.

37. Wiehl memorandum for Ribbentrop, September 22, 1941. IMTFE, IPS Doc. 4063, Item 11.

38. Groos to Ritter, December 29, 1941, GFM Files /1029/310457–61; and Wiehl to Ribbentrop, July 2, 1941, *Ibid.*, /21/13345 and /13346–60.

39. On the foreign-exchange factor, see Wiehl to Ribbentrop, July 23, 1942, GFM Files /21/13453–55; and Wohlthat to GFM, August 4, 1942, *ibid.*, /13525.

40. Wiehl to Ribbentrop, July 25, 1942, *ibid.*, /13475–77.

41. Wiehl to Ribbentrop, August 6, 1942, *ibid.*, /13538–40.

42. Groos memorandum, June 5, 1943. NWD.

43. The following is based on the two Japan folders from OKW, WiRüAmt Folder Wi/II c.3.3. and Wi/II c.3.4., and on company records, especially those of Rheinmetall-Borsig, Messerschmitt, Junkers, and Krupp. Also on interrogations of Japanese officers, IMTFE, IPS File 247–79; USSBS, *Interrogations of Japanese Officials* (Washington: GPO, 1948); and on a folder from the Japanese embassy in Berlin, Microcopy T-82/112 Item CD 969. Also on an American intelligence report, dated August 31, 1945, by E. G. N. Rushbrooke, made available at the Office of Naval

History. For help in the interpretation of the data, I am indebted to Colonel Thomas Everett Griess of the U. S. Military Academy.

44. Interrogation of General Walter Warlimont, OCMH, "German Staff Studies," MS # Ethint-4.

45. Wennecker interrogation in *Interrogations of Japanese Officials,* I, p. 284. Also Library of Congress, MS Division, "The German Submarine Materials," Box 370, "An envelope of material for the German naval attaché, Tokyo."

46. Jerome B. Cohen, *Japan's Economy in War and Reconstruction* (Minneapolis: University of Minnesota Press, 1949), p. 218.

47. The Germans admitted that much to the Japanese. Memo quoted in note 36.

48. OKW, WStab/Wi Ausl VI, "Vortragsnotiz für Chef W Stb," February 19, 1943, in OKW, WiRüAmt Folder Wi/II c.3.4. In December 1943, when the issue had not yet been settled, some Japanese urged that the Axis adopt a "lend-lease" arrangement. See memo by Adolf Steengracht von Moyland, December 6, 1943, on a conversation with the head of the German-Japanese Society. GFM Files /27/17477–79.

49. Ministry of Economics to Wiehl, V Ld 8/510/43 g Rs., February 8, 1943, in OKW, WiRüAmt Folder Wi/II c.3.3.

50. Wi Ausl VI c, draft memo, "Vortragsnotiz für Herrn Chef Wi St: Betr. Erwerb von Lizenzen, Nachbaurechten und Musterstücken durch Japan in Deutschland," February 23, 1943, in OKW, WiRüAmt Folder Wi/II c.3.4.

51. OKW, WWiSt (Ausl) 3. Abt., Az 3 i 39 IVb No. 2431/43 g, Schnellbrief to supreme commands, May 6, 1943, in OKW, WiRüAmt Folder Wi/II c.3.3.

52. Same to same, No. 4077/43 g of September 8, 1943, "Betr. Aushändigung von Nachbau-Unterlagen vor Vertragsabschluss," in OKW, WiRüAmt Folder Wi/II c.3.4.

53. Same to same, No. 264/44 gK, February 1944, "Betr. Japan–Nachbaurechte," *Ibid.* A copy of the agreement is in The German Submarine Materials, *loc. cit.*

54. Edward R. Stettinius, Jr., *Lend-Lease: Weapon for Victory* (New York: Macmillan, 1944), p. 50.

55. *Ibid.*, pp. 338, 342, for relevant sections of the Lend-Lease Act and the Russian master lend-lease agreement.

56. Ministry of Economics to Ausfuhrgemeinschaft für Kriegsgerät bei der Reichsgruppe Industrie and others, V Ld 8/4133/42 g of October 19, 1942. Microcopy T-71/118 Item RWM/27/80.

57. W. Stb Ausl/Ost IIb to 3.Abt IVb, "Betr. Einheitsvertrag der japanischen Wehrmachtstellen," April 12, 1943, in OKW, WiRüAmt Folder Wi/II c.3.3.

58. A copy of the master contract, apparently worked out by Reichsgruppe Industrie, is in Rheinmetall-Borsig files. Microcopy T-82, Serial 166, Folder 993/52.

59. Institut für Weltwirtschaft, Kiel, "Die wirtschaftlichen Kräfte Japans: Industriewirtschaft," July 1941. Microcopy T-82/92/248589 ff. Also USSBS, RG 243, Pacific War Report 52, Appendix.

60. Charles S. Popple, *Standard Oil Company (New Jersey) in World War II* (New York: The Company, 1952), pp. 9–11.

61. This and the subsequent reconstruction of the IG Farben story is based on company files now in the National Archives, Microcopy T-82. The material is in the following folders: Serial 82, Item GD 104; Serial 104, Items GD 307, GD 321, GD 322; Serial 105, Item GD 335; Serial 153, Item GD 936; Serial 242, Item GD 1386; Serial 245, Items GD 1559, GD 1582, GD 1835, GD 1836; Serial 246, Items GD 1563, GD 1774, GD 3014; Serial 263, Item GD 3044.

62. Büro Sparte I to director von Knieriem, August 9, 1940. GD 1835, Frames 2053192–95 and GD 1582, Frames 2046669–72.

63. IG Farben to Ministry of Economics, May 2, 1941. GD 1835, Frames 2052927–34.

64. IMT, Doc. NI-6925.

65. Decision after a conference between von Knieriem and

company lawyer Wolfgang Hentzeler, June 19, 1942. GD 1835, Frames 2052729–31.

66. Cohen, p. 136.

67. Dr. Pier to Dr. Bütefisch, June 8, 1943. GD 1386, Frame 2009693.

68. Bütefisch to Counsellor of Legation Nagai, August 5, 1943. GD 1386, Frames 2009733–36.

69. IG Farben minutes of a meeting in Ministry of Economics, Ausschuss für Nachbaurechte, November 23, 1944. GD 1386, Frames 2009571–73.

70. Copies, GD 1386, Frames 2009451–62, and in IMT, Doc. NI-6925.

71. My attempts to go over this story with participants still connected today with IG Farben's successor companies failed. One pleaded a bad memory, another refused to see me.

Notes to Chapter 5

1. *American Diplomacy, 1900–1950* (New York: Mentor Books, 1959), p. 66.

2. The German navy, presumably relying on Japanese data, assumed that Japanese sinkings in 1942 totaled 1.8 million GRT (Gross Register Tons). War Diary of the German Naval Attaché, Tokyo (Custody, Director of Naval History), April 10, 1943. Figures in S. E. Morison, *The Battle in the Atlantic, September 1939–May 1943* (Boston: Little Brown, 1947), Appendix 1(b), suggest considerably lower totals. In the Indian Ocean, Japan attacked British sea lanes to India, not the sea lanes to Africa and Persia.

3. See *Fuehrer Conferences*, 1943, p. 14, for discussion of the Japanese request. Decision in a memorandum filed in NWD, March 24, 1943.

4. Japanese claims for the first quarter of 1943 were 99,000 GRT. Because of Allied use of radar, Japanese sinkings probably declined hereafter. See War Diary of the German Naval Attaché, Tokyo, *passim.*

5. The offer of bases was made and accepted in December 1942. NWD.
6. *Ibid.*, April 17, 1943. Also Ribbentrop to Stahmer, May 25, 1943, GFM Files /27/17248–52.
7. Stahmer to GFM, July 28, 1943. GFM Files /1489/ 368757–58. On the Japanese-Italian conversations, see the German evaluation of captured Italian documents, *ibid.*, /131/70822–25.
8. For details, see Peter Kleist, *Zwischen Hitler und Stalin, 1939–1945* (Bonn: Athenäum, 1950), Chap. III.
9. The only evidence of Mamoru Shigemitsu's suggestion and Ribbentrop's interest I have come across is in Ribbentrop to Stahmer, February 13, 1944, IMTFE, IPS Doc. 4093, Item 7.
10. The German position is in Ribbentrop to Stahmer, September 4 and 6, 1944, GFM Files /1436/363340–42 and IMTFE, IPS Doc. 4093. The Soviet response is reported in Hattori, III, VIII, p. 305.
11. Hitler's explanation to Count Galleazzo Ciano, Italian Foreign Minister, December 18, 1942, in conference minutes, GFM Files /67/48160–216.
12. Kase, p. 165, note 15. A somewhat divergent Russian general staff estimate is in IMTFE, IPS Doc. 2237.
13. Ribbentrop, p. 248. That Hitler did not want a Japanese attack on Siberia is clear from his conversation with Raeder, October 27, 1941, NWD; from his talk with Oshima, January 3, 1942, IMTFE, IPS Doc. 4096; from his talk with Mussolini on April 29, 1942, GFM Files /67/47767–97, and from views of OKW which probably reflected Hitler's ideas. See Jodl statement to Nomura, December 4, 1942, and OKW WFSt situation report, December 10, 1942 (both in NWD), where similar views by the naval staff are set forth. Only by late July 1943 did the navy change its views; see marginal comments on report of OKH, Fremde Heere Ost, of July 29, 1943. OKH's views are in NWD, July 30, 1942, and memoranda filed there, of September 29, 1942 and July 29, 1943. As against this record, there is an occasional expression of interest in a Japanese attack on Russia, from Hitler himself in mid-July 1941 (see

DGFP, D, XIII, p. 141, editor's note) and from OKW in late December 1941 (Groos to Ribbentrop, December 24, 1941. GFM Files /1029/310575–76). The weight of the evidence shows the German leaders lukewarm or opposed, and confident they could destroy Russia singlehanded. By the time this view had faded, their confidence in Japanese strength had also been shaken, and they did not wish Japan to take on another opponent.

14. Ribbentrop to Ott, July 9, IMTFE, Def. Doc. 525-A. A Japanese reply in Ribbentrop-Oshima conference, July 27, GFM Files /67/48330–40, and in Hattori, II, IV, p. 121.

15. Oshima-Ribbentrop conference, February 19, 1943. GFM Files /1028/310304–19.

16. Siberian troops were employed on a significant scale in the December 1941 Russian counteroffensive, but did not enter the earlier fighting.

17. The Pacific route accounted for 47.1 per cent of all lend-lease shipments to Russia. Motter, Appendix A.

18. For the exchanges of May, see Foreign Minister Lutz Schwerin von Krosigk to Stahmer, May 6, 1945 (IMT, Doc. NG-4685), and a folder of their exchanges. Microcopy T-77/775/5501368 ff. On the Japanese press, see Robert Guillain, *Le peuple japonais et la guerre* (Paris: Juilliard, 1947), p. 233.

19. Klein, *passim,* and USSBS, *The Effects of Strategic Bombing on Japan's War Economy* (Washington: GPO, 1946), p. 15.

20. Interrogatory by General George C. Marshall, March 10, 1948, United States versus Ernst von Weizsäcker et alii, Weizsäcker Def. Doc. 415, Weizsäcker Def. Book VII, p. 22.

Notes to Appendix 1

1. The treaty text, in English in the original, and Ambassador Ott's letters are quoted from DGFP, D, XI, pp. 204–08. The treaty text was taken from the GFM Files, the Ott letters from the JFM Files, via the Tokyo trial (IMTFE).

Matsuoka's letters are quoted from a booklet with documentation on the pact negotiations, compiled in the fall of 1940 by the director of the treaty bureau, Shunichi Matsumoto, IMTFE, Def. Doc. 1656, pp. 165, 175, 161. English draft translations of these letters were provided in the Matsumoto booklet.

2. Jyo-ni, an abbreviation, stands for "Tr. 2"—that is, Treaty Department, second section. I owe this information to Mr. Mabuchi, formerly of the Japanese Embassy.

Note to Appendix 2

1. GFM Files /1029/310601–05. The peculiar formulation "United States of North America" is used throughout.

Bibliography

Unpublished Materials

German Records microfilmed at Alexandria, Va.; films deposited in the National Archives, Washington, D.C. For descriptions, microcopy numbers and serial numbers, see *Guides to German Records Microfilmed at Alexandria* (Washington: National Archives, 1958–). Material used came primarily from the records of OKW, OKH, Reichswirtschaftsministerium, and private German companies.

Captured German Records in the Federal Document Center, Alexandria, Va. Primarily records from the files of OKW, Wehrwirtschafts- und Rüstungsamt.

Records of the German Foreign Ministry. Microfilms in the custody of the United States Department of State, for the period September 1939–June 1940 and December 1941–May 1945.

War Diary of the German Naval Staff (*Kriegstagebuch der Seekriegsleitung*) for the war years. In the custody of the Director of Naval History, Department of the Navy. In compliance with navy policy, I have refrained from giving full and exact references to this material.

War Diary of the German Naval Attaché, Tokyo. In the custody of the Director of Naval History and with similar restrictions on source references.

The German Submarine Materials. The Library of Congress, Manuscript Division.

International Military Tribunal, Nuremberg. Files deposited in the Federal Record Center, Alexandria, Va.

International Military Tribunal for the Far East, Tokyo. Files deposited in the Federal Record Center, Alexandria, Va.

Office of the Chief of Military History, United States Army. German Staff Studies.

United States, Chief Counsel for the Prosecution of Axis Criminality. Files deposited in the National Archives.

United States Navy, Director of Naval History, report by E. G. N. Rushbrooke on Axis cooperation, dated August 31, 1945.

United States Strategic Bombing Survey, files in the National Archives.

United States of America versus Ernst von Weizsäcker et alii. Transcript of proceedings and documents in the Law Library, Library of Congress.

United States of America versus Wilhelm von Leeb et alii. Transcript. Law Library, Library of Congress.

Published Books, Articles, Serials

Only materials actually cited in the notes are listed here.

Assmann, Kurt. *Deutsche Schicksalsjahre*. Wiesbaden: Brockhaus, 1950.

Blau, George E. *The German Campaign in Russia: Planning and Operations 1940–1942*. Washington, D.C.: Department of the Army, 1955.

Bullock, Alan. *Hitler: A Study in Tyranny*. rev. ed. New York: Harper, 1962.

Cheng Yu-kwei, *Foreign Trade and Industrial Development of China*. Washington, D.C.: University Press of Washington, D.C., 1956.

Churchill, Winston. *Blood, Sweat, and Tears*. New York: Putnam's, 1941.

———. *The Second World War*. 6 vols. Boston: Houghton Mifflin, 1948–53.

Ciano, Galleazzo. *Ciano's Diplomatic Papers*. Edited by Malcolm Muggeridge. London: Odhams, 1948.

Cohen, Jerome B. *Japan's Economy in War and Reconstruction*. Minneapolis: University of Minnesota Press, 1949.

La délégation française auprès de la commission allemande d'armistice: recueil de documents publié par le gouvernement français. Vol. I. Paris: Costes, 1947.

Documents on German Foreign Policy, 1918–1945, from the Archives of the German Foreign Ministry. Series D, 1937–1945. Washington, D.C.: GPO, 1949–.

Drummond, Donald F. *The Passing of American Neutrality, 1937–1941*. Ann Arbor, Mich.: University of Michigan Press, 1955.

Feis, Herbert. *The Road to Pearl Harbor*. Princeton, N.J.: Princeton University Press, 1950.

Fuchida, Mitsuo, and Okumiya, Masatake. *Midway: The Battle that Doomed Japan*. Annapolis: United States Naval Institute, 1955.

Fuehrer Conferences on Matters Dealing with the German Navy 1939–1945. Washington, D.C.: Department of the Navy, 1947.

Fuehrer Directives and Other Top-Level Directors of the German Armed Forces, 1939–1945. Washington, D.C.: Department of the Navy, 1948.

Greiner, Helmuth. *Die oberste Wehrmachtführung, 1939–1943*. Wiesbaden: Limes-Verlag, 1951.

Grew, Joseph C. *Ten Years in Japan*. New York: Simon & Schuster, 1944.

Guillain, Robert. *Le peuple japonais et la guerre*. Paris: Juilliard, 1947.

Halder, Franz. *The Diary of Colonel General Franz Halder Covering the Period August 14, 1939 to September 24, 1942*. Washington, D.C.: Infantry Journal, 1947.

Hattori, Takushiro. *Dai toa senso zenshi*. [The Complete History of the Greater East Asia War.] Tokyo: Masu Shobo, 1953–56. Typescript English translation in Office of the Chief of Military History, United States Army.

Hilger, Gustav, and Meyer, Alfred G. *The Incompatible Allies: German-Soviet Relations, 1918–1941*. New York: Macmillan, 1953.

Hinsley, F. H. *Hitler's Strategy*. New York: Cambridge University Press, 1951.

Hosoya, Chihiro. "Sankoku domei" [The Tripartite Pact], in Nihon Kokusai Seiji Gakkai, Taiheyo Senso Gen'in Kenkyubu, ed., *Taiheyo senso e no michi: kaisen gaiko shi*. [The Road to the War in the Pacific: History of Foreign Relations on the Eve of the War.] Tokyo: Asahi, 1962–63.

Iklé, Frank. *German-Japanese Relations, 1936–1940: A Study of Totalitarian Diplomacy*. New York: Bookman, 1957.

Johnson, Chalmers. *An Instance of Treason: Ozaki Hotsumi and the Sorge Spy Ring*. Stanford, Calif.: Stanford University Press, 1964.

Jones, F. C. *Japan's New Order in East Asia: Its Rise and Fall, 1937–1945*. New York: Oxford University Press, 1954.

Kase, Toshikazu. *Journey to the Missouri*. New Haven: Yale University Press, 1950.

Kennan, George F. *American Diplomacy, 1900–1950*. New York: New American Library, 1950.

Kirby, Stanley Woodburn. *The War Against Japan*. Vol. II, *India's Most Dangerous Hour*. London: HMSO, 1958.

Klein, Burton. *Germany's Economic Preparation for War*. Cambridge, Mass.: Harvard University Press, 1959.

Kleist, Peter. *Zwischen Hitler und Stalin, 1939–1945*. Bonn: Athenäum, 1950.

League of Nations. *International Trade Statistics, 1938*. Geneva: The League, 1939.

Leighton, Richard M., and Coakley, Robert W. *Global Logistics and Strategy, 1940–1943*. ("The United States Army in World War II: The War Department.") Washington: GPO, 1955.

Lupke, Hubertus. *Japans Russlandpolitik von 1939 bis 1941*. Frankfurt am Main: Alfred Metzner Verlag, 1962.

Manstein, Erich von. *Lost Victories*. Chicago: Regnery, 1958.

Matloff, Maurice, and Snell, Edwin M. *Strategic Planning for Coalition Warfare, 1941–1942*. ("The United States Army in World War II: The War Department.") Washington: GPO, 1953.

Maxon, Yale C. *Control of Japanese Foreign Policy: A Study of Civil-Military Rivalry, 1930–1945*. Berkeley, Calif.: University of California Press, 1957.

Medlicott, W. N. *The Economic Blockade*. 2 vols. London: HMSO, 1952, 1959.

Menzel, Johanna M. "Der geheime deutsch-japanische Notenaustausch zum Dreimächtepakt," *Vierteljahrshefte für Zeitgeschichte*, V (1957), 182–93.

Monatshefte für auswärtige Politik. Hamburg.

Morison, Samuel Eliot. *The Battle in the Atlantic, September 1939–May 1943*. Boston: Little, Brown, 1947.

Motter, T. H. Vail. *The Persian Corridor and Aid to Russia.* ("The United States Army in World War II: The Middle East Theater.") Washington: GPO, 1952.

Musenberg, Captain. "Unbekannter Passagier auf U-180." *Der Frontsoldat erzählt,* XIX (1955), 181–82.

Nazi-Soviet Relations, 1939–1941: Documents from the Archives of the German Foreign Office. Raymond J. Sontag and James S. Beddie (eds.). Washington: Department of State, 1948.

"Opium, Erz, und Öle," *Der Frontsoldat erzählt,* XVIII, No. 8 (1954), pp. 246–47.

Popple, Charles S. *Standard Oil Company (New Jersey) in World War II.* New York: The Company, 1952.

Presseisen, Ernst L., *Germany and Japan: A Study in Totalitarian Diplomacy, 1933–1941.* The Hague: M. Nijhoff, 1958.

Ribbentrop, Joachim von. *Zwischen London und Moskau: Erinnerungen und letzte Aufzeichnungen.* Leoni am Starnberger See: Druffel, 1953.

Schroeder, Paul W. *The Axis Alliance and Japanese-American Relations.* Ithaca, N.Y.: Cornell University Press, 1958.

Sherwood, Robert E. *Roosevelt and Hopkins: An Intimate History.* New York: Harper, 1948.

Sommer, Theo. *Deutschland und Japan zwischen den Mächten, 1935–1940.* Tübingen: Mohr, 1962.

Stettinius, Edward R., Jr. *Lend-Lease: Weapon for Victory.* New York: Macmillan, 1944.

Trefousse, Hans L. *Germany and American Neutrality, 1939–1941.* New York: Bookman, 1951.

———. "Germany and Pearl Harbor," *Far Eastern Quarterly,* XI (November 1951), 35–50.

United States Congress, Joint Committee on the Investigation of the Pearl Harbor Attack. *Hearings.* 79th Congress, 1st Session. 39 parts. Washington: GPO, 1946.

United States Department of State. *Papers Relating to the Foreign Relations of the United States, Japan: 1931–1941.* 2 vols. Washington: GPO, 1943.

United States Strategic Bombing Survey. *The Effects of Strategic Bombing on Japan's War Economy.* Washington: GPO, 1946.

———. *Interrogations of Japanese Officials.* 2 vols. Washington: GPO, 1948.

Ward, Robert E. "The Inside Story of the Pearl Harbor Plan," *United States Naval Institute Proceedings,* LXXVII (1951), 1271–83.

Weinberg, Gerhard L. "Die geheimen Abkommen zum Antikominternpakt," *Vierteljahrshefte für Zeitgeschichte,* II (1954), 193–201.

———. *Germany and the Soviet Union, 1939–1941.* Leiden: Brill, 1954.

———. "German Colonial Plans and Policies, 1938–1942," in *Geschichte und Gegenwartsbewusstsein: Festschrift für Hans Rothfels zum 70. Geburtstag.* Göttingen: Vandenhoeck & Ruprecht, 1963.

Wheatley, Ronald. *Operation Sealion: German Plans for the Invasion of England, 1939–1942.* Oxford: Clarendon Press, 1958.

Willoughby, W. W. *Shanghai Conspiracy: The Sorge Spy Ring.* New York: Dutton, 1952.

Index

INDEX